MY PART TIME LIFE

HOW MY LONG LIST OF JOBS
HELPED ME GROW A
SIX FIGURE BUSINESS IN 365 DAYS

ERICA MARCHAND

◆ FriesenPress

One Printers Way
Altona, MB R0G 0B0
Canada

www.friesenpress.com

ISBN
978-1-03-915671-5 (Hardcover)
978-1-03-915670-8 (Paperback)
978-1-03-915672-2 (eBook)

1. *Biography & Autobiography, Business*

Distributed to the trade by The Ingram Book Company

Lauren, Freddie, Phoebe, and Tiffany

You don't have to have all the answers;
just don't be afraid to ask the questions.

INTRODUCTION

I ABSOLUTELY HATE name tags. To me, they are the epitome of lame, bestowed upon us by the corporate overlord called "The Man." I have detested them from day one. Not only do I think they look stoogey, they also have a tendency to wreck shirts. Even the magnetic name tags. Trust me, I know. Why, you ask?

I've had a lot of jobs. Like, a lot. And it took me a really long time to figure out "what I wanted to do with my life." I did fifteen years of grade school, six years post-secondary education, and have stumbled through all kinds of jobs. I've worked at fast food chains, golf courses, grocery stores, desk jobs, jobs where I'm on my feet all day, jobs where I'm valued, jobs where I'm underpaid, jobs where you desperately count on tips to make ends meet, jobs where my boss doesn't know my name, and I've even survived working with family.

I'm not saying I know everything about the workplace, because I'm sure my resume leaves much to be desired. But you know how they say you have to kiss a few frogs before you find a prince? Let's just say it took me twenty years of smooching the wrong prince before I realized that the prince was inside me the whole time. Okay, that sounded extremely inappropriate. What I mean to say is, I should've done some inward reflecting before puckering up to the corporate world of jobs.

They never taught us this shit in school. Oh, you have good grades?

Be a teacher.

Be a doctor.

Be an accountant.

Be a vet.

Be a nuclear physicist.

Be *something*.

It was never even suggested to be your *own* boss. That was never an option, which blows my mind because when I look around my small town, it is full of people who made that decision. They decided to pave their own way – take the leap of faith and invest in themselves.

Why aren't we teaching kids about how cool it is to be your own boss? To run your own business? To have the flexibility in your schedule to do what you enjoy *and* still get work done? To be able to set your own hours, not stress about whether your vacation time will be approved by HR or about that upcoming performance review. Do kids know that Apple wasn't always a billion-trillion-dollar corporation? It started with a couple of college dropouts brainstorming a better way to use and develop technology, and then they did it themselves.

My story isn't unique. There are many people out there who have had millions of jobs. It's job number 1,000,001 that really matters, though. When you decide to go your own way, Fleetwood Mac style and dive head first into entrepreneurship. It's absolutely pants-shitting scary (as long as you're wearing pants), but it's so worth it. The perks far outweigh the sleepless nights and premature greys.

I know plenty of millennials who had the same experience as me. I felt like I was destined for greatness, an excellent student, and somehow never truly Marie Kondo'd my way through life. No career ever sparked joy.

It can feel very overwhelming – that pressure of living up to everyone else's expectations of what they deem to be successful. I know. I've felt it time and time again.

There is that extremely toxic word that gets tossed around, especially by our elders: potential.[1] Potential is something people only discuss when you have so much of it but aren't using it. It's always mentioned in such a melancholy manner, too.

"Too bad he dropped out of college. Dave had so much potential."

Potential can put such an immense amount of pressure on a person. It took me thirty-four years to figure out what was driving me to be successful: that crushing weight put on me by family members, friends, teachers, employers, and above all else, myself. *Oh, hi anxiety, nice to meet you. My name is Erica, and I think we will be spending a lot of sleepless nights together reminiscing about all those times I failed to live up to someone else's perceived level of success.*

After starting my own business, I finally feel like I am starting to live up to that potential. It took me twenty years of working whatever job I could find, for whoever would pay me, to figure it out. I was never going to live up to the perceived potential I was carrying around if I was working for someone else. I needed to rely on myself to alleviate that stress. I asked myself: *Did I peak in high school? Am I ever going to have a career or am I destined to just have* a job?

When all your friends and family members have careers, and you're bouncing from job to job, it can be extremely deflating. Or even worse – when a high-school buddy who flunked out of college gets an incredible job and makes quadruple what you will ever make, you can feel your

---

1   Potential – the power to be epic or, rather, a nice way of saying, "You suck."

cheeks turning a nice, deep shade of green. Yeah, jealousy is a shit feeling. Oh, and here is our old friend Potential knocking on the door again. And look! They brought their BFF, Anxiety!

You do not have to try to fit into a cookie-cutter mould of what a successful career looks like. You don't have to find that job. You can *make* that job. It sounds cliché, but you can make a life you're happy and proud to live. You can make a name for yourself.

Like I said, it's pants-shitting scary. But in my experience, the community of entrepreneurs is unbelievable. Sure, there are some gatekeepers. There are in every industry. But there are some people and businesses out there that are willing to help build those up around them. I have had relationships grow and flourish because of the entrepreneurial spirit. Some of them are Instagram friends, while other relationships started as a business transaction and have grown into incredible friendships.

This book is here because I've had people help me on my journey, and now I want to help you. Or at the very least, open your eyes to what your life *could* be like if you took the plunge. You might feel alone, but you're not. There's always going to be someone to lend you a helping hand, even while you're still lying on the pavement fresh off a wicked wipeout.

This isn't a how-to book on how to start a business. Every business starts and grows in its own organic way. There is no one way to start, scale, or even maintain a business. Think of a business like a person. Everyone is different, unique, and has their own story[2].

This is the story of how I grew a six-figure business in 365 days. I hope I can help, teach, and inform some of you about how it happened, and how I took my part-time life into a full-time venture.

---

2   Amanda Marshall style.

IN THE BEGINNING

I WAS AN excellent student through school. I basically got straight A's in everything except math and geography (but that's what calculators and Google Maps are for, right?). I vividly remember sitting in my Grade 8 classroom and being handed a piece of paper with the daunting choice of whether to take academic or applied classes in high school. It was explained that applied classes were for college-bound kids (this seemed to have an inherent negativity around it, like that wasn't the right choice for a straight-A student to be making[3]), while academic classes were for university-bound kids. If you chose to take academic classes, you could always transfer down into the applied streams with no ramifications. But you would be fighting an uphill battle to transfer up to the academic level if you initially chose the applied classes.

This was the biggest decision of my life, or so it seemed. I selected academic for everything except math. I chose applied math because it was my weakest course, by far. My BFF at the time told me to erase my

---

3   Having gone to college twice in my post-secondary career, I can in fact argue that college was much more beneficial to me in every aspect of the word. The actual hands-on experience was second to none and helped propel me through my career paths faster than university ever did.

choice because "I was better than that." When I took the sheet home to my family, they agreed with her reasoning.

I've learned that I don't like doing things I'm not good at – like most people in the human race. I felt pressured to sign up for something that I knew was going to be an uphill battle. I felt defeated and scared. High school math … I could barely handle math through elementary school, so what would this new hell bring to me?

Fast forward to Grade 10 math class. We were learning about parabolas – super useful math that I use every day during tax season. I had studied my ass off and managed to flunk the test with a 43%. I was absolutely fuming, embarrassed, ashamed, and totally beside myself. Instead of sitting in a puddle of tears or silently banging my head against a wall, I exploded.

I asked the teacher when we were ever going to use this in real life. Hilarious, because what does a fifteen-year-old know about "real life." I snorted at her response and told her I thought that this class was bullshit. When she told me to go to the office, I dramatically exclaimed, "I'll never need this math, because I'm going to be an author!" I stood up and walked down the hall to the principal's office, face red and hot tears streaming down my face.

The principal was a pretty rad dude – and knowing I was a good student and being sent to the office was a rarity, he told me to just go outside and get some fresh air – one of the perks of living in a beach town. Thankfully, there were no consequences for my actions whatsoever.

When I think about it now, having to make a choice about your future at the tender age of thirteen seems so insane. If I could go back and tell Past Erica to take the college courses, I would. They were much more practical. I would've loved a course on practical math – like how to use a credit card or how the heck taxes work. I didn't know it at the time, but I was internalizing everyone's outward projections of what success looked like.

I craved those straight A's. I needed to be a well-rounded student because it was drilled into our brains that well-rounded students would be at the top of the list for post-secondary schools. I not only achieved an 85% average, but I did it while simultaneously playing basketball, acting in all the school plays, participating in the peer mentor group, being on the *Reach for the Top* team, and sitting on the student council two years in a row. I had referrals from my coaches and teachers about how I was a valuable asset to have at any university. Yet, when it came time to apply to my programs, I was never accepted. I was given alternate offers at all three universities. I had never been turned down before, for anything. It hurt.

I had done everything that everyone ever told me to do to "be successful":

- Take the academic courses
- Study your ass off
- Do all the extracurricular activities
- Smile

And it wasn't enough.

I identified as a well-rounded student. I wasn't the valedictorian, but I made up for it with my resume. I truly felt so deflated, like a party balloon that falls behind the TV unit after a party only to be found months later, wrinkled and hanging out with the dust bunnies.

This was the first time I felt like a failure, but it wouldn't be the last. I often left a job with that same feeling: defeat. It was much like the prince must have felt while touring the kingdom trying to find the perfect match for the glass slipper. I tried on lots of slippers, and none of them ever truly fit, until I tried running my own business. I didn't need a glass slipper – I needed Converse sneakers.

MY FIRST "JOBS"

I WANT TO preface this anecdote with the fact 16 year old Erica hated kids. Since I've had my own, and my friends and family members have had their own kids, I've grown to love them. The shit they say and do will make you laugh while simultaneously go grey young. They bring out the best, and worst in me – but teach me invaluable lessons. Seeing the world through their eyes, and the magic in the mundane that surrounds us is pretty damn cool. But Past Erica did not see that wonder. All she saw was an annoying liability. So, naturally, babysitting was a perfect fit.

I completed the babysitter's safety course in a room full of what Past Erica would lovingly describe as Keeners,[4] passed the course, and was now a fully licensed babysitter. It was a title I didn't overly love or want to advertise – again, kids. *shudders* But I did recognize I needed money so I could buy my own Ardene surprise bags at the mall, and not rely on my parents to foot the bill. It was the first step to that small taste of independence.

It didn't take long for my parents to start spreading the word to their friends that I could babysit. I never felt comfortable babysitting. Sitting in

---

4   Keeners: someone sitting on the edge of their seat, eagerly raising their hands for every question and giving off an entire "I know everything" aura. AKA brown-noser, ass-kisser.

8

a strange house, with strange food watching strange kids. Not my idea of a good time. I never jumped at the opportunity to babysit. Ever. More or less I would agree, in a ho hum manner, and begrudgingly spend my night wrestling a kid to bed. I was money motivated, but even with that light at the end of the tunnel, I tried to dodge the babysitting bullet as much as I could.

But you can't win 'em all.

My mom worked at the mecca for Northern Ontario fashion – Northern Reflections. She worked at a superstore that featured Northern Getaway, Northern Reflections, and Northern Elements.[5] My entire family was decked out in this gear. From Spice Mice, loons, Muskoka chairs on a dock, to howling wolves – we were the poster family for this company. I used to volunteer there with my mom when they had to change the seasonal merchandise- folding, steaming, and holding ladders. This was my first taste of a job, (even though I was only there because my mom didn't have childcare and wasn't comfortable leaving myself and my sister alone for that length of time). I was probably more in the way than anything else. But in my mind, they *needed* me there to help because it was such a daunting task to switch the store over. I actually liked the days she brought me into the store. It was a satisfying feeling, prepping the shelves and getting all the clothing folded and stacked neatly in a pile. I suppose ya'll would recognize this as foreshadowing to what my eventual career would be.

In hindsight, I learned how to balance work/life from my mom. She was a stay-at-home mom the first twelve years of my life. I fondly remember fresh pancakes for breakfast, homemade chocolate chip cookies in our lunches, and lots of nature walks. My mom is often referred to as Saint Louise, and whoever calls her that ain't kidding. She volunteered in the breakfast program in my elementary school, made all our Halloween

---

5   IYKYK

costumes from scratch, and somehow was able to manage the chaos that was my dad, myself, and my baby sis.

When we were young, we only had one family vehicle – an old, rusted-out Ford. When my dad worked night shifts at the gold mine, we would pile in the truck and drop him off at work and then come home and carry on with our night. My mom would then wake us up at the ass crack of dawn, load us back into the truck while half asleep and wrapped in our blankies, and go pick up my dad. I never remember hearing her bitch and complain about having to do this. She just did. She is so resilient and lets any worry roll off her back. Even though she's only 5'4", I look up to her immensely.

When she made the decision to return to the workforce, our lives were rocked. The matriarch of our home, the rock of our lives, was gone for eight hours of the day. Suddenly, I had to help around the house, including the task of making suppers – which normally ended up in disaster. There was one time I was cooking chicken breasts and forgot to turn the oven on and served raw chicken to my dad after a long day of work. Or that one time I cooked the chicken with the meat soakers still underneath them in the pan. Much to my husband's appreciation, my cooking has come a long way. Except that one time I tried to cook artichokes... Needless to say, it was a weird time in my life, with puberty and newfound responsibilities, but it taught me so much.

It taught me how to better manage time. If I needed to have supper ready for 5:30 p.m. when Dad got home, and it took an hour to cook, I needed to have my homework done by 4:15 to get everything in the oven. It taught me how to problem-solve. Even though my mom was only a phone call away, and I would call her many times a shift, I eventually learned that I could make decisions and figure things out for myself.

But back to the babysitting: My mom worked with a lady who lived around the corner from us. This lady asked my mom if I could watch her kids before and after school, Monday–Thursday. I rode the same bus as the two kids, so it kind of made sense. I would go to the house for 7:30 a.m. and get them on the bus. Then we would take the bus home, get dropped off at their place, and I would walk home around 4:30 when their mom got home. It was two hours of babysitting a day, no biggie. Or so I thought. I think about these kids a lot because they were nutso. The son was on prescribed medication that he refused to take, no matter how much I begged him.

The daughter used to eat butter. Just butter. Not on bread, toast, or crackers. One time, after chasing her brother around the house to administer his meds, I came back into the kitchen looking like I had just fought a jungle cat to see her crouching on the counter, Gollum-style, holding a brick of butter and taking massive bites out of it. Who were these kids?!

I can hear you now: *Erica, it was two hours a day, and you were getting paid to watch these kids.* Well, reader, you'd be more wrong than vinegar on french fries. (Don't come at me on this one. My mom used vinegar to clean the house when we were kids. When I smell it, my mind equates it to Windex or Pine Sol. When you douse your french fries in vinegar, you might as well be spraying Lysol on them. Also, it just doesn't taste good, and everyone knows that salt-and-vinegar chips are literally the worst kind of chips ever made. Ketchup, All Dressed, and BBQ are by far the superior flavours. THIS IS NOT UP FOR DEBATE.) But I digress – every Thursday, I'd collect my payment, and the mother would serve me a nice crisp purple.

Or two blues.

Or five twoons.

Or ten loons.

No matter which form the payment came in, it was always the same total amount: $10. That's $1.25 an hour. For all you youngins reading this, yeah, 1999 was a simpler time, but the minimum wage was $8.92. Here is some quick math: if I was being paid minimum wage, I'd be getting paid $71.36 a week, which is vastly different from $10.

I did this for a few months, even though I complained about it openly to my mother. I loathed going there. I hated not knowing if the boy was going to cooperate, or if the butter Gollum would come crawling out of her cave hunting for her next dairy meal. I eventually told the mom some lie so I didn't have to babysit one weekend. (She would ask me to babysit the occasional weekend when she had to work at the mall.) Spoiler alert: since she worked with my mom, I got caught in the lie. It felt awful – not one of my best moments, but I didn't know how to tell her I hated baby-sitting, that her kids were wild creatures, and, frankly, that she wasn't paying enough.

LIFE LESSON: KNOW YOUR WORTH

When I started Bear+Fox Apparel, I felt guilty charging people for the product I was selling. Read that again. I felt *guilty* for charging people for the product I was *selling*. This is pure insanity. The product wasn't free for me, but I felt like it should be free for everyone else. Why? Because I was doubting my ability and the viability of my business. Not only did I feel bad telling friends and family how much a sweater would cost them, I also set my prices too low. My margins were minimal, and the profit was essentially nonexistent.

This continued for a few months until I received some feedback that my prices were too high. Too high? *Too high*!? I wasn't making ends meet with the prices I had set, and this consumer thought I was overcharging! That's when I had my Aha Moment:

You're not too expensive;
you're out of their price range.

After that feedback, I decided to set my prices at a place that I figured was fair from a consumer standpoint and allowed me some wiggle room in terms of margins.

As the business has grown, I believe more and more in the product and the brand as a whole. I am completely comfortable with my price point and have no problem charging friends and family for the product too. This is a great reason to have a website. I direct everyone there to order their products, which removes me from the process and therefore metaphorically duct tapes my mouth from offering any sort of discount.

> **Know your worth, and don't waiver from it, because you're worth every penny.**

MY FIRST REAL JOB – HARVEY'S SERVING SWISS CHALET

MY HUSBAND WILL laugh at this one. He always chuckles because I refuse to just call it Harvey's. It was more than a Harvey's ... it served Swiss Chalet, for Pete's sake!

I was thirteen, and my parents gave me the age-old ultimatum: "You want to go to the movies? Go get a job and pay for it yourself." It sounds harsh, but it was true. At some point, you have to cut the umbilical cord and understand the value of a dollar. I'm still not so sure I fully understand it, but we will get there.

So began my foray into the absolute worst kind of hunting ever ... job hunting.

I applied to a few spots around town, and the Burger Bar was one of them. I even got an interview! I was pretty jazzed to get an interview, considering I had no work experience. They either really needed help, or I totally wowed them with my empty resume. Regardless, they wanted me to memorize the menu and know it inside out and backwards before I showed up for the interview.

As much as I wanted a job, I wasn't convinced I wanted a job there. But beggars can't be choosers. I half-ass studied their menu. I couldn't keep the toppings straight between the bacon cheeseburger, cheeseburger, burger,

15

nate burger. So, I totally bombed the interview. I remember
s from the lady interviewing me, breaking out into a nervous
ght-up guessing if a burger had mustard on it or not. And I
very vividly remember *not* caring. It was a greasy dive bar with a staff over
the age of thirty, which was old. (Cut me some slack, I was thirteen, okay?)

This was the first time I failed in the real world. I was upset, but
not surprised.

LIFE LESSON: YOU GET WHAT YOU PUT INTO IT.

I often get questions about how I get the opportunities I do with regards
to my business. For instance, when Canadian rock band The Glorious Sons
were wearing my gear in their promo poster for their summer 2021 tour,
or Sharon from the famous trio of Sharon, Lois, and Bram posted a story
wearing my shirt, or when Tim Rozon from *Schitt's Creek* was wearing
the appropriately named LongJohnny Rose – people want to know how I
did that.

And my answer is always the same: I did the damn work. I reached out
and asked these Canadian icons if they would be interested in some free
shit. I curated items I thought they would actually *want* to wear, based
on their style. I work my ass off to find opportunities and make myself
available for them. You know what they say: There ain't no rest for the
wicked … or the self-employed.

The interview process for the Burger Bar taught me that hard work
gets rewarded – and in that case, I probably would have been rewarded
with a job if I had done the work. But I didn't, so I didn't. I've taken that life
lesson and applied it to my business. I work on my business every damn
day. Whether it's designing new clothing, outsourcing blanks, networking, social media content, picking up and organizing stock, packing orders,
delivering to my wholesale accounts, creating marketing campaigns,
booking meetings with my bookkeeper, participating in lectures/classes

to improve aspects of the business or even writing a friggen book- there is something to do every day. The thing about owning a business is you might not see the return on your investment right away. It might take days, months, or years for all your hard work to pay off. But it will, in some way or another, it will.

I couldn't leave the Burger Bar interview a total loser that day. So instead of leaving with a job, I left with a purpose - I needed to find a job and fast. My friends were going to the movies and living their best lives with everyone on the big screen. I wasn't going to be joining them any time soon if I didn't have a job.

If my life had been a movie, I would have been walking down the sidewalk. Rain pouring down, and me without an umbrella. I'd look in the window of the movie theatre and see my friends buying their popcorn and laughing obnoxiously over jokes that aren't that funny. And the musical score would be Coldplay's "The Scientist"... *"Nobody said it was easssehhh ..."*

Surely there was a place in town that would love to employ me. I just had to find it.

My dad drove me out to the other end of town, resumé in hand. I was dressed in black dress pants and a white-collared shirt, as was the traditional resumé-drop-off attire. I left my resume at a grocery store, two big-box stores, a video rental store,[6] a pet store and lastly, Harvey's Serving Swiss Chalet.

When I dropped off my resumé at Harvey's, I recognized some of my classmates there. I felt intimidated. It's a weird feeling, the feeling of Have-Notness. All these people in this restaurant had what I wanted ... income. It felt like such a clique. All these people had a job and subsequently a paycheque, financial freedom – independence. I needed what they had.

---

6   R.I.P Blockbuster.

I can't remember the exact time frame, but for the sake of dramatic effect let's say Harvey's was so blown away by my resumé filled with metaphorical moths and tumbleweeds that they called and demanded an interview the very next day (or something to that effect). I was absolutely terrified. Considering my first interview didn't have the desired outcome I wanted, this seemed like a second chance. This could be my first *real* job! I was shaking in my knock-off Vans.

Now, I want the jury to note that I don't condone lying. I think honesty is the best policy and being authentic is the only way to live. It's one of my core values, and something I attribute to my success as a business owner. But what I did in preparation for this interview is either pure genius or ranks me up there with some of the most insane sociopaths out there. (Why, hello, Ed Kemper, I'll be your room mate this year at Boarding School!)

I wanted money, but I knew I did not want to work every weekend. Although I didn't know much about the working world, I did know what seniority was. And I knew I was going to be at the bottom of the scheduling food chain. I wanted some cash flow, but I'd be damned if I was about to give them my entire weekend. So, I did the only thing a girl could do. I went to Ardene's and bought some earrings. But not just any earrings. Oh no ... these were tiny gold crucifixes. I had a game plan.

The next day, as I prepped for my interview (which consisted of my dad asking me stereotypical interview questions and me staring at him blank-faced as I tried to answer them with some degree of intelligence), I donned the internationally recognizable I-have-an-interview outfit (which is almost identical to the I'm-dropping-off-a-resume outfit). I made sure to leave my studded belt and choker at home, after all, I had an image to uphold. I centre-parted my hair and pulled it back into a big-ass clip, and I applied some too-heavy eyeliner to my lower lash line, smeared on some of the quintessential 2002 mascara (you know, the pink tube with the green lid), lined my lips with some cherry ChapStick, and put in my earrings. I think I heard my skin sear when I put the holy metal through my ears.

I was ready.

When I got dropped off at Harvey's Serving Swiss Chalet (I will never *not* call it that), I had the nervous farts. My guts were turning. After completely bombing the interview at the Burger Bar, I needed to turn on the charm and nail this interview. I could not fail again. I almost thought about running in the opposite direction, but I'm not a chicken shit. Also, my dad was in the truck since he was my ride home, so I didn't have much of a choice.

I was offered a drink, which I declined and then instantly regretted because I suffered from cotton mouth the whole time. My mouth was dry, palms were sweaty, knees weak, arms were heavy – I was nervous. Marshall Mathers style.

During my interview, which was held in the dining area of the restaurant, I not-so-subtly would tuck my hair behind my ears. The owner probably thought I was nervous, which I was. But I also had an ulterior motive.

The owner was telling me about how they were flexible with student schedules, as students made up a majority of their staff. She explained that they worked hard to make sure everyone was able to complete schoolwork or participate in extracurricular activities, if there was enough notice. She then asked me if there was any time off that I would need. I looked her dead in the eyes, tucked my hair behind my ears, and said, "I would like Sundays off so I can go to church." I had never been to church in my life. Okay, that is another lie. See! Once you start lying you cannot stop. I had gone once in Brownies and fell asleep in the pew.

As the words tumbled out of my mouth, I could feel my face get red. Or was it the crucifix burning through my ear lobes? Did I even look like I went to church? Should I have worn a habit? Referenced *Sister Act II?*

Should I have done that motion where you say, "Spectacles, testicles, wallet, and watch?"

I was floored when she said it was not a problem. I could exhale. I did it. I lied and did not get hit with a bolt of lightning, and I actually got what I wanted. I was hired on the spot. I was so stoked!

LIFE LESSON: ASK FOR WHAT YOU WANT

This is something that, yet again, I learned early in my foray into the working world that would benefit me in my small empire.

I have learned that I am tenacious and that I truly listen to my gut. If there is something I want, I will point blank just ask for it. My thought process is that worst-case scenario, the answer is no. Best case, the answer is yes and a door is opened.

As a business owner, especially a sole proprietor, you are your only advocate. You need to stand up for what you believe in and what aligns best with your business and your brand. I have turned down partnerships or collabs because they do not serve my business in a way that will help it grow and evolve into the brand it has the potential to be. Sometimes this can put you in some uncomfortable situations. You will have some awkward conversations where egos and feelings will be hurt, including your own. That's okay.

You need to protect your business like it is your baby. You did not put the time, effort, and money into your business just to watch it get bulldozed by other influences. Advocate for yourself and ask for what you want, or subsequently, do not want. Opportunity is often just on the other side of the question.

Did I love my job in fast food? No. But at that point in my life, loving it was not a necessity. I had a paycheque, and I loved the people I worked with – save a few cranky supervisors who probably hated working with teens. I mean, I get it. Us teens were living our best emo lives and were probably annoying as hell. This job was my leg in the door. The very first addition to my resume.

I still call it Harvey's Serving Swiss Chalet because it was more than just a fast-food joint. We were a bunch of kids learning shit about "the working world" while balancing social lives, school, and sports teams. Oh, and we served chicken too.

THE APPLIANCE STORE

I DO NOT remember why I left Harvey's. I do, however, remember being very happy I wasn't going to smell like deep-fried potatoes at the end of every shift. Showering immediately when I got home from work was a must because I felt like a walking french fry. I knew I did not want to work in fast food, or maybe even in the restaurant industry at all, so I totally changed courses and shotgunned my resumé across town to every business that didn't serve food.

Somehow, I landed a job at an appliance store that was also a pick-up location for a national catalogue. I would lose sleep over this job. One of my main responsibilities was balancing the till at the end of the day, which I never managed to do. It literally caused anxiety. I would feel this bubbling of emotion starting to overcome me throughout my shift, anticipating the moment I would sit down to try to balance the till. I vividly remember the stress of calculating all the numbers and tallying all the receipts to find I was over/short money. I hated that I could not do this seemingly simple task. I felt like a moron. It didn't help my anxiety with math and numbers either, if anything, it fed into that insecurity.

I truly believe this is where my anxiety towards money festered, grew, and followed me through adulthood. Maybe if the math we were being taught in school was not always algebra and trigonometry, we wouldn't feel these negative emotions when it came to "real life" math. As a business owner, I understand the importance of balancing your books and understanding where your money is going. Starting Bear+Fox Apparel actually helped me and my relationship with money – understanding how it ebbs and flows and being able to predict how my next quarter will go has helped me in my personal life as well.

The appliance store was not always stressful. When the shop was opening, we would have to drive the riding lawn mowers to the road for display ... so naturally, me, Joe, and Cat Scratch would have epic lawn mower races. We would come barreling out of the trailer on our lawn tractors driving like Shriners in a parade – chirping each other as we drove with the pedal to the metal to get to the parking spot first. They were great co-workers. We shared the same sense of humour and taste in music. When our boss wasn't there, we would play Weezer or Tenacious D while we were closing up shop and just rock out, using vacuums as guitars, and power sliding up and down the aisles. Days when the owner was not there were always good days. Days when she was there caused premature greys.

I liked her as a person, but the job and the work environment were not ideal. She would often roll her eyes when I could not find the appliance model she was searching for. She would lose her cool when I couldn't balance the till (which I understand – it's her business, and I'm sure it looked like I was either completely incompetent or stealing money). But I think what stands out the most from this job is that she would call me Shelley. She would yell across the store, "Aww, piss, Shelley!" or "Shelley, you drive me to drink!" The smallest mishap and I would hear her cursing "Shelley!" Which was somehow, me. To this day, if someone is driving me nuts, I call them Shelley. What can I say? We take a piece of these experiences with us through life. Calling ding-dongs Shelley is something I have adopted and will never give up. If I call you Shelley, you know you done effed up.

I worked there for a couple years, and it ended in a hail of bullets. It was the day after prom, and I was not in the best of shape. But I was there. It was a rough day, both physically and emotionally. My boyfriend and I had recently broken up, and obviously I was hungover. I think I was finally reaching a breaking point at the job. I needed something else, something where I felt appreciated and competent. I did not like feeling dumb and useless at work. As an excellent student and overall good kid, this job was messing with my confidence and self-esteem.

I was sweeping the floor, and she called out for a stove by the model number, which I hated because I could never find it in the small, crammed loading dock. After a half-assed attempt, I told her I could not find it. And then she said it: "Shelley, you drive me to drink!!"

I flipped shit.

I yelled that my name was Erica, and she could find the fucking stove herself.

I think I saw her pupils dilate and the steam come out her ears. She jumped over the counter so fast, and I turned and booked it through the loading dock. We were climbing up and over boxes of lawn mowers, stoves, fridges – everything. I clawed my way to the back door and grabbed my bag and car keys. I got to my mom's red Chevy Sunfire and opened the door to hear her scream, "If you get in that car, don't bother coming back!"

I turned and looked at her, with the wind blowing through my hair like Nic Cage in *Con Air*, and said with conviction and authority, "I'm never coming back. I fucking quit."

I know she was yelling and screaming something, but I didn't hear her. I was already in the car and on my way home. When I checked in my rear-view mirror, she was doing her best Yosemite Sam impression and stomping the ground and waving her hand in the air. I felt so liberated and free. It was all adrenaline because I had never said those things to an adult before, let alone my *boss*.

I got home and my mom looked at me and asked if I was home for an early lunch. I said, "No, I just quit … or got fired, I'm not too sure on the details." My mother, the consummate roll-with-it queen, shrugged and said, "Guess you better print off some resumés."

LIFE LESSON: DON'T STRESS ABOUT WHAT HAPPENED – MOVE FORWARD.

I easily could have stewed over the way I left this job. There were plenty of emotions rolling through both myself and my boss when I burned out of that parking lot. We can't stew on what has happened – but we can use it to move forward.

This is something that keeps my business rolling full steam ahead. There will always be situations or issues that arise that are not ideal. Maybe it's launching a product that you think will fly off the shelves, but it collects dust for over a year, and you end up liquidating it at cost to recoup your cash. Maybe it's your website crashing. Maybe it's a marketing campaign that you thought would blast your business into the stratosphere, but it has extremely low ROI[7] and essentially results in zero sales. Maybe it's having your Instagram page hacked, deleted, and lost forever in the dark web.

Fun fact – all of these things happened to me within a two-week time frame. Shit happens; you don't have to stand in it. Take these lessons or opportunities and allow your business, mindset, and operations to shift and regroup.

Allow yourself to feel the feelings. It's your gift with purchase when things go sideways. Oh you lost your Instagram account? Here, have

---

7   Return on investment

some anger and frustration to go with that. And hell! We'll throw in some embarrassment as well! Situations like these tend to be paired with icky feelings, like shame, embarrassment, rage, sadness, that feeling of stupidity, failure. Utilize those feelings in a way that will allow you to change the narrative.

My Instagram account was responsible for 91% of my online sales. When it was hacked and deleted, I felt absolutely devastated. Everything I had worked so hard for, and on, for the last two years was just gone. After the initial shock and shame associated with falling for a phishing scam, I decided to use that moment to really examine my business and decide what I wanted from it. I made the conscious decision to see this experience not as a loss, but as a gain.

I shifted my branding ever so slightly and really niched down into a market that I was barely scratching the surface of with the initial branding I was using for the business. This slight shift helped push my business into the best month to date and has allowed more like-minded individuals to find my business. Subsequently, it has helped grow my reach, and increase sales.

> **Shit happens, you don't have to stand in it.**

THE GROCERY STORE

I GOT HIRED at three places at once after my "exit interview" at the appliance store. I had no clue what I wanted to pursue, so I accepted all three jobs. I was not jazzed on working at a grocery store, but again, I just needed some cash flow. I was very much money motivated, and arguably still am. Which is ironic because entrepreneurship is not a "get rich quick" plan.

I worked at the grocery store for one month. I was a terrible employee. If I did not know the produce someone was buying, I just punched it in under the "miscellaneous" code and charged the person ten cents. I hated the entire atmosphere. The onboarding for this grocery store was minimal. I basically got thrown onto a cash register and told, "You figure it out." I felt like a fish out of water, totally stranded on an island full of mystery fruit. The things people bought that I had never even seen or even heard of before, was wild. Dragonfruit, starfruit and prickly pears were all a first for me. So naturally they all fell under the "misc" 10 cent charge.

I got taken off the schedule there because my boss thought I called her a slut.

DISCLAIMER: I DID NOT CALL HER THAT.

I had another job during this short employment at the grocery store, and I left a voicemail with the hours I had scheduled at the Pizza Hut. Apparently, it sounded like I was calling her something else. Bad reception, maybe? No idea. (I learned all of this from an employee that did the sched-uling when I asked why I wasn't getting any shifts.) I don't even know if I made enough money to cover my forest-green work polo.

LIFE LESSON: ENUNCIATE

That's it. Be clear when you speak because you want to say what you mean and mean what you say.

THE PIZZA RESTAURANT

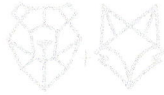

THIS WAS MY second foray into what would become a long career in the food industry. I did not think I would be back in this industry after I left Harvey's Serving Swiss Chalet, but this wasn't fast food. This was a sit-down restaurant, and there were tips involved. I was super stoked to work there. Not only because the pizza restaurant was a safety net when I got taken off the schedule at the grocery store, but because there was a server there that I had performed with in school plays and looked up to immensely. I was glad to be able to work with her, and as cheesy as it sounds, I hoped maybe some of her badassery would rub off on me. Plus, the restaurant was around the corner from my parents' house, so I could easily walk to work. During the one-month stint that I had worked at the grocery store, the pizza place was also only a couple blocks from there, so I could easily commute between the two places on days I worked a double. But we all know how that ended up.

(Again, *enunciate*.)

It wasn't overly glamourous, and the tips were no hell. But it wasn't rocket science. I learned quickly and had fun doing it. It was the first place I could serve beer, which I loved to do, although I did pour more pitchers of pop than beer there. It catered mostly to families and hockey teams full of kids. I hated lunch buffets with a fiery passion. The payout from a lunch buffet would be next to nothing and was hardly worth the time. But thankfully, since I was in school, I rarely worked these. I mostly got the evening shifts.

On my best night in tips, I got $180. Ironically, I also got a ticket that night for a traffic violation for $180, which I spitefully paid at the county office in all my tip change. Stickin' it to The Man, one dime at a time.

It wasn't the best serving job, but it was a great introduction to the world of tips and bartending. It also opened my eyes to the service industry. Not just the serving aspect, but the comradery that is really built and formed in the kitchen, and the hierarchy of positions within the restaurant as well. Restaurants are really built from the dish pit up. I truly think everyone should work at least one restaurant job in their life to really understand everything that goes into creating a night out.

There were some tables that I genuinely liked serving. We would share some jokes during our time together, and it almost didn't seem like work serving them. Even if you dumped an entire tray of drinks on them, they somehow were still pleasant and friendly. (Yes, this actually happened, and yes, it was trés embarrassing.)

And then there were the nightmare tables. I had someone at a table ask me, point blank, if I was stupid. I remember feeling totally humiliated by them. They talked down to me the entire interaction with them. I started my shift at 5'8" and could feel myself shrinking down to a measly eight inches as the night went on. After dealing with their derogatory and rude comments while I took their orders and brought them refills on their pop, I walked into the kitchen and shed a few tears while I collected myself to bring them their pizza. Shawn was working in the kitchen and saw how upset I was and told me to wait on serving their pizza because he forgot a key ingredient. Ignorance is bliss in this situation. I'm not 100% sure what he added, but I know he had a big shit-sniffing grin on his face when it was served to them.

LIFE LESSON: BE KIND TO EVERYONE

This is a fun one. As you can tell – I've had many jobs, very few of which had any kind of clout or power associated with them. I was rarely a supervisor or manager and often worked, in some form, in the service industry. I've had people be extremely kind, and I've had people treat me like I'm a literal servant, a less-than, and not worth their time or kindness. Now that I have a successful business, podcast, and some social media influence, I am finding some of these people are slowly making their way out of the woodwork.

I'm not saying to channel your inner elephant and never forget, as that can be a slippery slope and can have some negative side effects on your own mental health/well-being. However, how people treat others when they don't seem to fill a need, speaks volumes about their character, morals, and values. You need to ask yourself: Is that something or someone I want to be affiliated with? I'm willing to bet it's not.

When I first started Bear+Fox Apparel, I wanted to get the brand and logo out there as much as possible. Similar in how I would shotgun my resumé across town, I would partner with anyone who wanted to give my business the time of day. As my business grew, I learned that I was allowed to advocate and choose whom and what I aligned with.

What makes the most sense for my business? Does it make sense to partner with a business/brand that sells vegan products? A fishing lodge? An MLM[8]? A business/brand with a strong political stance? Like I said before, it makes for some uncomfortable conversations, especially if you have some sort of history/relationship with the person, but you need to protect your assets, and one of those assets is your reputation.

If you are affiliated with a person/business that treats others with poor integrity, cruelty, and snideness – your business will be reflected in the

---

8   Multi-Level Marketing

same light. Be cautious. If you're approached by a new potential partner/collab, don't be afraid to ask around in the community and see what their reputation or vibe is. Again, advocate for yourself and your biz. If you don't fight for your business, who will?

Like I said, working in the restaurant taught me how tight a work family can be. The family can also be absolutely insane. We've all seen *Hell's Kitchen* – and sometimes it's a true depiction of what kitchens can be like. I've worked in a few where I witnessed many screaming fights between employees. Oh, and if you took an order from a table and there was a long list of modifications on the order? May God have mercy on your soul if Andrew was working. Because there would be pots and pans thrown out windows when he saw that chit. IYKYK.

I worked there for a year or so. I eventually didn't love the atmosphere created by one of the managers. Hindsight, maybe she was not as bad as I recall, but I was also a high-school kid, and she was at least in her forties. We had different values. For her, this was a career – it was paying real bills. For me, it was just a way to make a buck while I was saving for university. Also, I learned that I maybe didn't want to work for a franchised business. After working at Harvey's Serving Swiss Chalet, and now the pizza place, it seemed like corporations were not where my heart was, but it was something I would do again to really reiterate that notion.

THE STORE THAT SELLS BEER

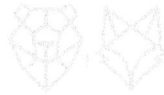

I WORKED A short while at this place in Ontario where you can buy beer. I think I only worked there a few months while I juggled the pizza joint and the grocery store. Having three jobs at one time is a lot to manage. PLUS, you know, school.

While I was doing the onboarding process, I had to watch a few slide-shows and complete a few quizzes. I'll never forget the uniform/attire section. It was very clear on what you could and could not wear to work. It had one particular piece of clothing that was not permitted. I had to ask my boss about it. I said, "Bert? Did someone actually show up to work in a beer-branded bikini top?"

He laughed and shrugged. "If they have it written in the manual, then someone did it somewhere!"

It still blows my mind – because he's right. Rules are made because somewhere, someone did something. Or in this case – wore something.

It was a pretty decent gig. There were some gross aspects, like dealing with returns. People would bring in empties that they had stored in their garage for what must have been eons. I distinctly remember seeing a dead mouse in a few bottles, some tampons, and of course, cigarette butts. These are all fine and dandy when they are in bottles, as those don't get tossed into a bin. They get sorted and stacked in boxes and flats. But the cans? Let's just say, if you smoke darts, don't use a can as an ashtray. I've been the girl on the other end of the recycling chain who tosses the cans in a big plastic bin. I've been covered in stale beer and cigarette butts more times than I care to admit, and it's just nasty.

LIFE LESSON: YOU WON'T LOVE EVERY ASPECT OF YOUR BIZ

I love my business – clearly, or I wouldn't want to spend my days writing about it in this book. I love the opportunities it has granted me, my friends, and my family. I love the flexibility it has afforded me with my children, the immense amount of satisfaction I get when I hear the Shopify cha-ching when a sale is made, and the creativity I get to use for designing the gear, content creation and photoshoot prep. I love most aspects of my business. But there will always be parts you do not love.

For me, it's the accounting/bookkeeping. I know you just read that and threw this book across the room like, "What the hell does this chick know about growing a business if she doesn't like the part that actually determines if she's grown a business?!"

Let me explain.

It's no secret that I'm crappy at math. I've been telling you that from page one. I've struggled with it most of my life. I will literally use a calculator for any simple math problem. I lack the confidence in my skills and abilities to maintain accurate books. I knew this early on in my business venture. It created stress, anxiety and multiplied my grey hair overnight.

When I saw the sales creep up towards the limit where I would need to start charging HST, I knew I needed help. This was no longer just a side gig; this was a legit business. I was referred to a bookkeeper who wanted to specifically help women-led businesses learn how to balance their books. I met with Kathy and we vibed instantly. She has a no-bullshit, the-numbers-don't-lie attitude – and I loved it. As much as the numbers gave me instant anxiety and made me want to pour a whiskey just to cope with the sheer amount of panic, she was there to talk me off the ledge and show me how to navigate the back end of my business.

I vividly remember her walking me through how to compile my monthly reports on a zoom call (we were still in a Pandemonium[9] at the time.) While I was sitting there, fighting back tears of frustration because I felt totally overwhelmed watching her effortlessly punch in numbers in an Excel spreadsheet, I heard the poof of my little Shoulder Angel and Shoulder Devil. While they normally are on opposite ends of the moral spectrum, they were both in wild agreement on my plan of action here.

I burst out and asked Kathy if I could just pay her to do the things she clearly loved, and I could do the things I clearly loved, and we could meet once quarterly to review the numbers and ensure everything was on track to hit our goals. She agreed, and I have been much happier ever since.

> **Know your strengths and play into them. Know your weaknesses and compensate for them in a way that makes you feel comfortable and accomplished.**

Meeting once a quarter always causes me a bit of stress, because again, numbers – but having my books in the capable hands of someone I trust allows me time to breathe and focus on making money, not necessarily managing the money.

---

9   I'm over calling it what it was. I never want to hear that P word ever, ever again.

THE FIRST GOLF COURSE

I APPLIED TO the golf course when I realized I did not want to work in the corporate world. The pizza joint and beer retailer were the epitome of corporate. I needed some change. I applied to a locally owned golf course. This is basically the same as applying to work on the moon. I did not golf and had zero intention of ever learning how to golf. I find it one of the more insane and mundane sports out there. I do not know how people *watch* it on TV – I'd rather chew glass. But my tactic when applying to jobs was that I liked to shotgun my resumé out into the universe to see what stuck. I guess the golf course was sticky enough because I got hired as a banquet staff/halfway-house girl.

I loved the halfway house. It was great! I was working alone slinging hot dogs, egg sandys, and beer. What more could an eighteen-year-old girl ask for? I rocked out to some bangin' mixed CDs, which were heavy on The White Stripes, Weezer, Heart, Kelly Clarkson, The Strokes, and of course, Journey. For the first time in my resumé-building adventure, I was working totally independently from anyone else. It was just me and my boom box, surrounded by hot dogs and beer. Life was grand.

LIFE LESSON: INDEPENDENCE IS FREEDOM

This was the first job where I really got the taste of working alone, which now, as a one-woman show, I do daily. Learning how to time manage at a young age has really helped me build my business. There are days that simply just slip away on you, especially when you have kids.[10] It goes without saying, I love my kids, but girrrl have mercy because they can derail a day faster than you can say "Thomas the Tank Engine."

You need the ability to alter your schedule around your responsibilities, and you need to be able to prioritize the never-ending to-do list. I was able to learn quickly what needed to be done first at the golf course, so I could continue with my day in a way that made sense. I use these skills now when I sit down and create my weekly plan. I break everything down month by month, week by week, and then day by day. I tend not to get too specific in the hours spent on a task. Again – operating a successful business around children is an adventure. If I can check everything off my list by the end of the week, I consider that a success.

> **Do not stress about the "work/life balance" bullshit that everyone is obsessed with obtaining.**

If you are striving to have that on a day-to-day basis, that just will not happen. Period. I like to look at it on a yearly basis. At the end of the year, I will reflect on the gains my business has made, the adventures my family has had, and where I am at personally, mentally, and physically. Did I reach

---

10   Crotch goblins, sex trophies, ankle biters, liabilities, kiddos – whatever you choose to call them.

my sales goals? Did my family check everything off our NYE list[11]? If the answer is yes – then I achieved work/life balance.

I did not love the banquet/events aspect at the golf course. Serving food was not the part I didn't like. It was the clean-up. Everyone would leave from the tournament, wedding, or event and then we were left cleaning up. Clearing tables, stripping linens, and doing dishes. This was 2005 and, for whatever reason, we hand washed all the banquet dishes. HAND WASHED. Before you get all "millennials don't know real work" on me, think about it. 200+ salad plates, 200+ meal plates, 200+ dessert plates, 200+ coffee cups and saucers, and the never-ending stack of cutlery. This does not include the dishes used to actually MAKE the meal. The granny of the golf course would sometimes come in to wash the dishes, and we would dry and put them away. She liked her water so hot; I have no idea how her skin did not melt off her hands. She told us, "The hotter the water, the faster the dishes dry."

LIFE LESSON: GRANDMAS DON'T WASTE TIME IN THE KITCHEN.

Learning that the dishes could air dry a little bit before we took a towel to them saved on the number of towels (and subsequent dirty laundry) needed for every event and truthfully cut down on the wages the employers were spending on the night. It allowed us to work more effectively in the kitchen. While we were giving the dishes an extra minute to air dry, we were able to get the kitchen and dining area cleaned up, as opposed to

---

11   Instead of creating New Year's resolutions, we write down things to do in that upcoming year. For instance, we had a list of twenty-two things to do in 2022. Some things on the list include catching newts, sleeping in a tent, swimming in five lakes, cooking a pizza over a campfire, and eating out at five new restaurants. It's satisfying to check things off the list while simultaneously making memories with my family. Forget losing that twenty-two pounds – gain twenty-two memories.

waiting until all the dishes were done to get started on that task. Working smarter, not harder, is the cousin to multi-tasking. They seem to carpool to family events together.

Once dishes were done, there was a list of closing duties to be performed in the clubhouse. All the banquet staff would basically divide and conquer this list so we could GTFO ASAP.[12]

I'll never forget this one outrageous night I drew the short straw to clean the bathrooms. You had to clean the toilets, wipe the counters, ensure that all the soap and toilet paper was well stocked, empty the garbage, Windex the mirrors, and mop the floors. Nothing wild. Oh, and whoever was cleaning the bathrooms would also mop the hallway in the basement as well. Again, not a huge deal, and most nights it was no biggie. Most nights.

The women's bathroom was always in immaculate shape, but the men's was a gamble – it could be okay or a nuclear disaster. There would inevitably be mud prints, no matter what the weather was. It was seriously almost commendable how their shoes always seemed to find mud on the course, even in the middle of a drought in July. They could never seem to get the paper towels in the garbage and inevitably there would be piss on the toilet seat. Oh, and the smell. There was ALWAYS a smell.

So, I went down into the basement to clean the washrooms, and I started in the women's. I hammered that easy task out. I mopped the hallway floor down to the men's washroom and then I smelled it … I took a deep inhale and went into the mouth of the beast. Or the ass – because this smell should never be associated with a mouth. EVER.

I ran around picking up all the paper towels off the floor and chucked them into the garbage. I speed-wiped the mirrors and counters. Checked the soap dispensers and then kicked down the door to each stall and gave them a fast swipe with the toilet brush. There were five stalls.

---

12   Get The Fuck Out As Soon As Possible

Boom, door one. TP supply: full. Piss on seat: minimal.

Boom, door two. TP supply: full. Piss on seat: maximal.

Boom, door three. TP supply: minimal. Piss on seat: minimal.

Boom, door four. TP supply: adequate. Piss on seat: inevitable.

Boom, door five, and there was the stall causing the horrendous odour molesting my nostrils. I was gagging. But there was absolutely nothing in the toilet bowel. It was pristine. Almost … too clean. I scanned the TP sitch and noticed it was a completely empty roll with the sad party streamers grasping onto the brown cardboard for dear life. I did a quick peek around the back of the toilet for any stray shits and found nothing. But my nose hairs were burnt off, and I was starting to lose vision. There was *something* there. I noticed the water level in the toilet seemed to be too high, so I reached to the back of the toilet and pulled off the lid.

And fucking ran out of there so damn fast.

I sprinted upstairs, gagging, tears streaming down my face from the pure stench and rallied the troops. No one was going to believe this. I needed reinforcements, and we grabbed what we could find to cover our faces – dish towels, napkins, and even some golf socks from the pro shop. With my banquet buddies at my side, we all trekked downstairs into the bog of eternal stench.

I led them to the stall that was basically emanating green stench-steam lines like we were in a Looney Tunes sketch, and I opened the door. One by one, all my coworkers went into the stall and basically fell back out coughing, gagging, and laughing hysterically. There, in the back of the toilet, was a literal shit storm. Some grown man had shit his boxers and stashed them in the back of the toilet. I do not fully remember how they got out of there, but I do recall tongs.

LIFE LESSON: BE KIND TO YOUR SERVERS.
THEY LITERALLY HAVE TO DEAL WITH YOUR SHIT.

For the rest of the season, I side-eyed every male member of the golf course as the potential Boxer Bandit. The culprit was never found, but it did happen one more time. Thankfully, not when it was my turn to clean the bathrooms.

There was one time the beer cart girl couldn't work the "celebrity tournament." Now remember, I don't live in LA, so the celebrities at the tournament weren't anything crazy. I remember them mostly being NHL refs and local nobodies.[13] Having a golf tournament without a beer cart is basically golf-course suicide, so I was bestowed the task to water the troops for the day.

I had no idea about the layout of the golf course. Like I said, I don't golf, never will golf, and quite frankly, don't like golf. I was driven around a couple times on a cart to get a feel for the route. In typical Erica fashion, I did not pay attention. "I'll just follow the cart path" was the flawed logic I was working with. But the cart path was not clearly marked everywhere. Sooo ... I essentially just made it up as I went. *Que sera sera*, right?

I was told not to go too fast or the cart would dump. (Again, my ears are just there to help hold up my hats and earrings.)

I went fast.

And I dumped it.

Ice everywhere.

It was also a super loud crash. Which meant I would have to get creative answering the question "What was that noise on 7?" which my bosses asked when someone inevitably complained they did not make the shot

---

13   Somehow "local nobodies" seems to include lots of radio DJs, who love to hear themselves talk.

because of the ruckus. It couldn't possibly be because they were just not a good golfer. No way, Jose!

There was one particular spot where you couldn't see the tee from one hole, and you had to creep out to see if someone was teeing off. If there was no one, you would book it across to the next hole. Well, I was creeping up and did not see anyone at the tee. I slammed my foot on the gas and started to book it out from behind the bushes. POW!

I got fuckin' nailed with a golf ball on my left thigh. I instantly fell out of the cart and landed on the ground. It was *so* sore. I scrambled back into the cart and took off like a bat out of hell. Gerald and Linda (the owners) were not going to like this.

When I got in the clubhouse at the end of the day, Gerald asked if there was anything eventful that happened on the course. I lied through my teeth as he eyed up the purple welt on my thigh. He gave the obligatory "I'm disappointed" look over his glasses and continued on his way. That ended my beer-cart career.

I worked at the golf course for three seasons. But as all good things must come to an end, I was let go in a truly millennial manner. I was sitting in my university dorm chatting with the owner's daughter on MSN about when my exams were done and how early I could come back to the golf course for the summer, and she told me they did not need me anymore. Yeah, over MSN Messenger. I basically changed my status to:

°°¤ø,¸¸,ø¤º°`°°¤ø.uNeMpLoYeD°°¤ø,¸¸,ø¤º°`°°¤ø.

THE CONSERVATION AREA

AFTER GETTING FIRED on MSN Messenger (which my university roomie will never let me forget), I was starting to feel the all-encompassing freak out about where I was going to work for the summer. I thought I had my summer all planned out to work at the golf course, but that was not going to be the case. My friends all seemed to have their summer jobs lined up. I felt like I did back in high school, watching my friends all go to the movies while I sadly walked through the rain listening to Coldplay. So, in true Erica fashion, I sent my resumé out everywhere. I had a couple interviews and then finally landed a job at a conservation area as a youth counsellor. It was advertised as a job for someone enrolled in a post-secondary program specializing in early childhood education and, I mean, English and pop culture is close enough, right?

I did not even like kids, ya'll know this about me by now, but it checked a bunch of boxes for what I was looking for in a job. It was Wednesday to Sunday, 8:00–4:00, which was great. I was young enough that I could still party on the weekends and not be completely hungover and useless for the next day. Ahhh, to be young and indestructible. I got Mondays and Tuesdays off, which were spent at the beach with my bestie who had a serving job and typically had weekdays off to hang by the lake. It was a damn good summer.

I got to don another forest-green polo, although this one had a different vibe from the grocery store polo. It was very "park ranger" in design, and I *loved* it. Plus, I kind of pulled off the look with my khaki flood pants and aviators.

The job was fairly flexible in terms of duties. Every week, I would lesson plan on a theme and then offer activities for the kids in the park. We learned about eco systems, specific habitats and animals, food chains – whatever! Although truthfully, I did not do much lesson planning; I just used the plans leftover from the over-achiever who had the job the year before.

LIFE LESSON: WORK SMARTER, NOT HARDER

If you are able to think of an easier way to accomplish the same output, do it. It could be a collaboration with someone who has a design team willing to take the reins on a project, or it could be partnering with an Instagram account that has a much higher engagement rate/reach and allowing them to post a giveaway with your merch to increase your social media following. Or it could simply be using lessons planned from the previous year, so you have more time to actually spend with the campers (or reading the newest Harry Potter book while you're on the clock). There is always another way.

> **Use the thing on your neck.**
> **It's not just a hat holder.**

My duties were essentially being a nature nut and sharing all that knowledge with the kid campers in the park. I was basically Smokey the Bear without the lame costume. And let me tell you, growing up in

Northern Ontario, I basically had all the knowledge needed for the job. When you grow up in an outdoorsy family, you just pick up on lots of tidbits of information. To this day, my useless knowledge of frogs, turtles, snakes, and other animals is usually met with excitement from my kids and their friends.

We hosted a family-fun fishing derby one weekend, and my job was to walk around the pond, take photos, and help the kiddos out when they needed it (baiting hooks, helping them if they caught a snag, unhooking fish, etc.). I measured the fish and recorded the length/weight and generally helped out that day. One kid caught a decent fish, brought it over to the scale, and asked what kind it was. I said, "Well, that's a perch," and explained all of its identifying features – the separated dorsal fins, stripes down the side, oval shape, and the yellow/orange tinge to the belly. The head ranger said that there was no way there was a perch in the stocked pond. I adamantly argued with him that it was a perch. He checked the records, and wouldn't ya know, there were a handful of perch released in the stocked pond in 1975 and not one had ever been recorded being caught. So yeah, Jason, I know what a fuckin' perch looks like.

I actually loved this job. When I look back at all the random jobs I have had, this was the closest thing to what I wanted to be when I was younger. A family friend, who is like an uncle to me, worked for Ducks Unlimited, and I would always hear about these cool adventures he would be on in the bush. When everyone was dreaming of being marine biologists, I was dreaming of working for Ducks Unlimited in their swamp division (is that even a thing?) and catching and cataloguing frogs. Not to toot my own horn, but I am a damn good frog catcher. And yes, I can catch more frogs than anyone. Challenge me, I dare ya. To this day, if there is a pond with frogs, snakes, turtles, newts, and other aquatic critters, I'm in there like a dirty shirt. You don't get a nickname like "Critter" by sitting on the river-bank. Needless to say, this job was fulfilling all my childhood dreams.

I did not stick to the lesson plans religiously. If kids showed up to the trailer, I was expected to teach them *something*, and since I did not have a direct supervisor and was working independently, I would make a judgement call on what the daily activities would be based on the kids who came to the trailer. Most of these kids were city kids who had never held a frog, crayfish, or snake. I would make them all trek down to the river, and we would spend the morning catching critters and talking about them. THEY LOVED IT. Watching them collect a bucket of crayfish and then talking about what they eat, where they live, what eats them, and inevitably how hard they can pinch always made for a fun day. It rarely felt like work. It was something I genuinely enjoyed doing. I take every chance I get these days to teach my kids and my friends' kids all about nature and the cool animals that live around us. Spending my summer wading in the river was a great way to make money.

One day, I had a group of about five kids, and I decided to go to a different spot to catch some aquatic critters. We walked by the falls and talked about how the water level was high because we just had a heavy rain. If there was a really hot week, the falls would run dry and subsequently not make for a great vacation, considering the conservation area was literally named after the waterfalls. We continued walking the shore and then hit a spot where we needed to hop on a rock to avoid a low-hanging branch. I stood in the water and helped the kids jump across on this rock.

One kid jumped and made it to safety.

Then another.

Then another.

Then the fourth and the rock blinked.

PARDON ME? My heart sank as I noticed the rock we were using as a trampoline was a fucking massive snapping turtle. It was like something out of *Jaws*. The camera zoomed in on my face like I was Chief Brody and the music started playing.

Daaa Da … Daaa Da …

The fifth kid jumped and landed on the turtle, and it was glaring … if looks could kill. And all I could think was, "I can *not* return this kid to his parents with one less toe."

Da Daa … Da Da … Da da da da da da …

The kid leapt to land and the snapper just slowly walked away and faded into the murky water at the waterfall, where boatloads of people were swimming. I shrugged. That was not my problem. As long as I returned these kids to their parents with all appendages, I was good. Jaws lived at the base of the falls for the summer and was spotted only occasionally by some swimmers. No one died or lost a toe (that I know of) that summer.

That summer I saved a Gatehouse Girl from a big-ass garter snake; I trapped and released a bat that was sleeping in my windows on the trailer; I enjoyed lazy afternoons walking the river banks catching aquatic critters; and I spent an entire rainy shift reading *Harry Potter and the Order of the Phoenix*. When we hosted a car show, I got to drive a 'Stang around the park (thanks to a generous entry in the car show trusting me with her sparkly pride and joy).

I was stoked to work there the next summer, but ultimately, I was not offered the job again. They found out I was not actually enrolled to be a teacher post-secondary so … back to the summer job drawing board.

LIFE LESSON: ALWAYS TELL THE TRUTH BECAUSE IT WILL EVENTUALLY CATCH UP TO YOU.

THE DISPATCH JOB

AFTER NOT GETTING hired back at the conservation area, I was yet again caught in the worst hunting season – job hunting. I was constantly searching newspapers and online databases, and I was dropping resumés off at places uninvited. My mom eventually found a posting for a summer student at a trucking company whose head office was only a forty-minute drive from St. Catharines, where I went to school, so I could easily go there for an interview instead of hauling ass all the way back home.

I remember sitting in a big conference room, with a big table and dozens of cushy chairs, freezing in my pencil skirt and blouse (another take on the quintessential interview garb). It was fairly intimidating, considering my interview experience was mostly comprised of sitting in someone's office one-on-one. This felt like I was going to be interviewed by a board of executives. I was not 100% sure what this company hauled around Ontario, but hey, I was Erica! I could figure it out.

I was interviewed by the owner and his two children (whom the business was named after) along with the office manager for the office I would be working out of, should I be lucky enough to land the position. I charmed them with my smile, humour, and overall demeanour, and only fibbed once when they asked if I was proficient in Microsoft Excel. I smiled and told them absolutely, which was a total crock because since I was an English major, the only exposure I had to Excel was how to spell the word.

LIFE LESSON: FAKE IT TIL YOU MAKE IT – AND YOU CAN LITERALLY GOOGLE ANYTHING.

I am a very firm believer that you can figure anything out as you go. Google is an incredible tool that we all have at our fingertips. If you need to differentiate gross, net, and revenue – you can Google it. If you need to figure out the average price for a sweater in Canada, Google it. A recipe? Google it. Who framed Roger Rabbit? Literally anything.

When I started my business, I had serious anxiety and stress about not having all the answers. As the business owner and the overlord in the Bear+Fox universe, I thought I needed to know everything from the beginning, but it felt like all I had were questions.

How do I launch a website?

How do I figure out my margins?

How do I charge appropriately for shipping?

How do I, how do I, how do I...

The reality of the matter is that you do not have to know it all to launch a business. You just have to be ready, willing, and able to find the answers you need, when you need them.

I have always had an attitude of "Say yes now, figure it out later." I have had Zoom calls with a national beer brand in regard to a potential partnership. Do you think I knew everything leading up to those meetings? Absolutely not. I had no idea what we were going to chat about. Was it about a co-branded brew? Co-branded merch? Social-media collabs? Or was it just a friendly Zoom call to get on each other's radar for potential future partnerships? I had no clue. But I accepted the invitation and showed up ready and willing to learn. I Googled the ever-loving shit out of this company. I bought a case of beer – which helped in the research process.

No, seriously. Not only did I get a sense of their branding on their cases, but I was also able to study the cans too. After cracking a couple bevvies for myself, I dove into their online presence and took notes on what I thought could align well with Bear+Fox.[14]

Did I have the answers? No. Was I willing to get them? Yes.

And that willingness got me a seat at the table across from a national brand – one that could catapult my biz into the stratosphere.

But I digress. I got the job. It was ten-hour days, 7:00 to 5:00, and it paid more than my friends were making in their other jobs. I was elated. My first office job, a true rite of passage.

It was not overly glam, by any stretch of the imagination. I was the only girl in the office, so the washroom was always a fun adventure.[15] I probably suffered from PTSD from the golf course bathroom, but there were days I thought about going home to use the washroom for peace of mind. Besides the utilitarian washrooms, the actual job itself was not very glamourous either. I basically just input numbers into an Excel spread-sheet (which I did not have to create, thank God) and took messages for the office manager. It was not very stimulating.

I licked envelopes, Seinfeld style, for an entire day. And I spent the days on MSN Messenger with head office if I had any issues with the data I was inputting. (If MSN Messenger does not date me, I don't know what will.) This was at the beginning of social media; Facebook was the only heavy

---

14   At the time of this publication, I'm not at liberty to disclose the beer brand or the potential outcome of this meeting. But you can learn more by following Bear+Fox on all the socials.

15   The Boxer Bandit never made an appearance here.

hitter around at the time, and many of my friends still used MSN to chat. So, I would spend my free time sending Cracked.com articles to my buddy Scott and planning my weekends at the beach online.

I was also obsessed with reading celebrity biographies and decided to use my time in front of a screen to write a book. Yeah, I'm that person who writes a book on company time – which I guess I'm still doing, except now the company time is paid by yours truly. I also printed the book off and used their paper and ink. It was called *The Girl with the Hearty Laugh: Autobiography of a Nobody.* I still have it printed on my shelf at home. I cannot even bring myself to read it; it was more of a diary than a book I'd ever want to publish. But it gave me a project for the long ten-hour days.

I was under-challenged, and frankly, not needed in the office. The office manager did everything and was not ready to relinquish any responsibilities to a summer student. I understand. I do. It seemed to be a recurring theme in my summer jobs: businesses hiring students to help with the workload, but then not being ready to hand over responsibility to the summer student. But holy shit, was I bored. We listened to a lot of Alan Cross' "Ongoing History of New Music." When I hear his voice, I am transported back in time to a small, dusty office space and an old desktop computer.

There is literally no exciting story from this job. That is how boring it was.

LIFE LESSON: IF YOU'RE A SOCIAL PERSON – FIND A WAY TO BE SOCIAL AT WORK, EVEN IF YOU WORK ALONE

I am a solopreneur. I work for myself, by myself. There are days that I am totally alone and do not speak to anyone until I pick my kids up from the bus stop. I've always enjoyed the social aspect of work – getting out of the house and seeing/talking to people. The lunch breaks, the coffee runs, the "smoke breaks." When you work alone – somehow the lunch breaks are not as exciting when there is no one sitting across from you at the table. The coffee runs to the kitchen don't come with office banter and the "smoke breaks"… well they don't happen because I don't smoke.

This is where my social media comes into play.

I allow myself time to chat with people in the DMs. I share a part of my day and then I engage back with followers, consumers, and community members. It allows me to have a small sense of coworkers throughout the day. Because, between you and me, my boss can be a bit of a spin chisel at times.

I worked in the office for two summers, and then I left. I needed something more. Very specifically, I needed human interaction. Working in a small office space with zero contact with humans outside of the office manager was making me go cuckoo. And you know what Johnny says, "All work and no play make Jack a dull boy."

THE PUB

THE NEXT SUMMER, I decided to expand my search by looking outside of my town and applied to a bougie pub the next town over. Serving is not rocket surgery, and once you've done it once, you can do it anywhere. I nailed my interview and got the job. SPOILER ALERT – I can carry a few plates and remember orders without a pad and paper. I was going to be working alongside some new faces, such as people who lived in that town as well as some classmates I did not know well because we didn't do the same extra curriculars.

It was an *excellent* summer. The tips were magnificent, and the work was hard, but it was chock full of social interaction, exactly what I needed after my summers in the office world. I learned so much about all the fun beers we had on tap and how to serve with a slightly elevated style opposed to the serving jobs I had had before. Working with people I didn't have much of a relationship with during high school was refreshing. It was almost like making new friends. The servers all became close that summer, which speaks to the comradery in the serving/kitchen realm.

There were stressful days in which I took up smoke breaks. You read that correctly. I did not take up smoking, but I took up smoke breaks. You see, if you are a smoker, you get these random fifteen-minute breaks throughout your day to go smoke a dart. Since I didn't smoke, I found this colossally unfair. Harkening back to my silver crucifix earrings, I bought a pack of cigarettes and kept them in my locker. When I had a stressful day, or just needed some breathing space (the irony is not lost on me here), I would claim I needed a smoke break and go outside. I would light a cigarette and just let it burn between my fingers. When it was out, I'd go back inside and continue on my day.

LIFE LESSON: FIND THE LOOPHOLE

I am proudly Canadian. When I'm at a Blue Jays or Maple Leafs game and the national anthem plays, 10/10 I'll be shedding tears. Watching Canadian athletes at the Olympics; the range of terrain this country offers – from the prairies, the oceans, to the Great White North; listening to Canadian artists around a campfire; there are so many moments and things I love about this excellent country. I needed this to be included in my brand.

When I had my supplier/printer price out 100% Canadian products, I think I dry heaved in our meeting. Straight-up retching sounds while trying to save face in the board room. The prices are *insane*. As a start-up, I could not justify carrying Canadian products – unless I wanted to charge upwards of $150 for a sweater. I did not think anyone would spend that amount of money on a product from a start-up business. Once there is an established brand voice and expectation of quality, then that price can slowly climb. Look at lululemon. They can charge $100 for a pair of yoga pants because there is the quality and the branding lifestyle associated with the brand. I was a nobody. I had one follower (thanks, Mom!) and no brand awareness.

It was extremely important to me to support Canadian products as much as possible. And that's when I found "the loophole." My products are supplied by a Canadian company, designed locally, printed/embroidered locally, and Bear+Fox is obviously owned and operated in Canada by a Canadian. So, where is the loophole?

The products are supplied by a Canadian company, but they are not specifically made or fabricated in Canada. This was a tough pill for me to swallow, but it made the most sense for my business. It allowed me to have better margins on my products while I grew brand awareness and the business in general. Bear+Fox Apparel has aspirations to become 100% Canadian.[16] Every business needs goals to work towards – and this is proudly mine.

One weekend while working at the pub, I was serving a couple on their honeymoon. They were such lovely people. They didn't tip overly well, but I overlooked it, partly because they were on their honeymoon, and partly because they were just enjoyable to serve and be around. At the end of the weekend, they asked if I had any plans for the following weekend. Now, I watch a lot of murder docs. I'm a certified murderino, so my spidey sense was tingling. They were either going to murder me, kidnap me, or ask me to join them for a threesome. I wasn't getting total creeper vibes, but everyone thought Bundy was a cool dude too. I told flippantly them that my boyfriend and I were heading to a concert in Toronto.

The groom tilted his head and asked, "At the Molson Amphitheatre?"

I nodded.

"Oh, for the Brad Paisley concert?"

I slowly squinted my eyes and nodded, with a slow "yesss" escaping my lips.

He told me he was the professional photographer for the venue and gave me his number, saying, "Text me when you're there."

I called Corby, my then-boyfriend, now-husband, who is 6'10" and basically a human shield. I told him that I was going to text this guy as maybe he had a hook-up for us or something.

---

16   This would be far more attainable if large businesses in Canada sourced their products domestically as well. Until the big guys do this, it makes it next to impossible for the little guys to source Canadian-made products. It's just a fact of life.

On our way to Toronto, I sent a text to the groom. He texted back immediately, telling me to text him once were in the venue. We parked, scanned our tickets, and I texted him while we were waiting in line for an overpriced beer. He told us to meet him by the side stage lounge. We walked over, and he ushered us into a private bar with big-screen TVs everywhere and cushy couches with lakefront views. He apologized that we would have to watch the first two acts from there, but once Brad took the stage, he was going to come and get us and move us up from our nose-bleed seats. Best tip ever? Absolutely.

I met Jason Blaine backstage,[17] we drank overpriced and overrated beer, sat on over-stuffed couches, and felt like total rock stars. Everyone in the lounge was staring at us. Not because my husband is 6'10" (which is why people normally stare, ha!) but because they had no idea who we were, and everyone in there was someone important.

I still think back to that concert and how surreal it was. All because I could carry a tray of drinks and bring food to a table.

LIFE LESSON: EXPERIENCES ARE WORTH MORE THAN MONEY

That was not the only thoughtful tip I got at the pub. I was working on my birthday, and it came up in conversation with a table. I mentioned that I had a collection of salt and pepper shakers at home, although why (on both accounts) this came up in conversation, I'm not sure. I brought the bill to the table, and when I turned around to bring the debit machine, I noticed cash on the table. They had tipped me one dollar. My ass was chapped for sure. I thought we had a good vibe the whole time, and for them to tip only one dollar, I felt skunked. To add salt to the wound, *it was my birthday*. But

---

17 Literally ran up to him while he was talking to an exec at CMT and said, "Hey Jason! It's me, Erica!" As if he should know who I was. Corby still laughs about it. Now when we are in social situations and I don't know people, I'll always introduce myself that way, and we have a good laugh about it.

this is what happens as a server: you win some, you lose some. However, you normally have a good inclination when a table is not going to tip well based on the hour you spend with them. I cleaned their table and continued my shift. It was fairly dead, so I got cut. Not in a stabby knife way, but in a "you can go home" way. I finished my duties and moseyed up to the bar to have a post-shift bevvie and count my cash out.

This woman burst through the door to the pub like a tornado in July. She came shuffling over to me and slammed a gift bag on the bar. "This is for you," she huffed. I recognized her as the woman from my One-Dollar-Tip Table. I opened it, and there was a cute pair of ceramic turtle salt and pepper shakers. I smiled and looked at her. She simply said, "Happy birthday," and walked back out the front door. Working on your birthday can be a lot of fun. It's a special day, and work just slaps different. But it can also really slap in a not-so-fun way.

ANOTHER CRABBY CHAIN RESTAURANT

ANOTHER SUMMER JOB, another waitressing gig. I worked at this chain restaurant because a couple girlfriends had worked there the summer prior and said they made killer tips. It was down the street from my house and would save me driving to a different town. (I did not have my own car, so coordinating my schedule with my sister and parents could be a nightmare at times).

There was one particular Sunday that I'll never forget. It was my birthday again. But not just any birthday, it was my champagne birthday. I was twenty-two on the twenty-second. This was a birthday I had been planning in my head forever. Champagne for everyone, party at the beach, a private concert by Kid Rock (don't come after me for it, he has some real bangers!) followed by more champagne and a campfire on the sand watching the sunset. Yeah, I wanted a bitchin' champagne party. Little did I know, it would be significantly less cool than the rager I imagined in my head.

I went into work for my shift and was overly perky ("hello, it's my birthday!") but very swiftly had my metaphorical birthday balloons popped.

A party of four sat in my section. There were two adults and two kids, which automatically means the bill would be only half of what it normally would be, since the kids would be eating for free: one of the promos this chain restaurant proudly advertised for every Sunday. I approached the table, took their drink order (four Cokes, surprise) and gave them some time with the menu. When I returned with the drinks, one lady ordered for everyone at the table, which I found strange, but whatever. You do you, man. She ordered two kid's meals (shocker), fajitas, and a burger. When I brought the fajita shells and the cold condiments/dressings to her table, I stated I would be back with everything else. The alpha female rolled her eyes while scowling. Which, if you try to do, is really quite hard. When I brought the skillet with her peppers, chicken, and onions sizzling on it, she looked utterly disgusted, saying, "What? You're not going to put my meal together for me?"

When I explained that fajitas were served like this and that the customer gets to put the fajita together however they would like, she seemed completely baffled and inconvenienced. I do not think this is unique to this restaurant – this is literally how fajitas are served everywhere. Google it.

This table kept me *huss-sa-liiin'*. Every time I did a table check, they needed something, and instead of asking or treating me like an actual human being, they were fetching me around. I managed to keep a smile on my face and pep in my step. The faster I could get this table served and out the door, the sooner this façade would be over, and I could finally exhale.

I also firmly subscribe to the notion that you can kill anyone with kindness.

When I came back to check on how everyone was doing, she just stared at me. I refilled their Cokes and cleared their dishes, after she told me it was "disgusting" (even though she ate literally every bite). If you have worked in a serving role, this is a joke often told to servers in a sarcastic manner when the plates are licked clean. I gave a smile and probably made some smart-ass comment like, "I can tell!" and walked their dishes to the dish pit.

I returned and took the kids' dessert order (because you eat like a damn king for free on Sundays so long as you're under twelve!) and the alpha female also wanted dessert. She ordered chocolate cake.

Back to the kitchen I went to make the kids' sundaes and plate the cake. Spoiler alert, this is not fresh cake. It's a frozen slice of cake: think ice-cream fudge cake. We just pulled it out of the freezer, put it on a plate, and drizzled some chocolate sauce on the plate to make it look less like a cake you just pulled from the freezer and more like a piece of artwork.

I brought out the desserts, smiled, and said, "Enjoy!" and before I could even turn to leave, the alpha female said, "What is *this* on my plate?" I looked down. With her tone you would think there was a cockroach or, God forbid, a hair on her plate.

I did not see a thing. "I'm sorry? What am I looking for?" I asked. She pointed her long, witch-like finger to a fingerprint on her plate. A fucking *fingerprint*. I looked at her, totally confused. "It looks like a fingerprint," I explained, as if I was speaking to a toddler.

"Why is there a fingerprint on my plate?!" She started raising her voice. At this point, since there were other patrons in the restaurant, people were staring at us. I could feel my face flushing. Not because I was scared of her, but because I could feel The Erica starting to bubble to the surface.

Now, I have been known to drop the occasional F-bomb from time to time. I come from a long line of "sentence enhancing" French Canadians. We use "fuck" like commas. Through my years of job experience, and functioning in society in general, I know to keep the cussing tucked away while I'm at work. Smile and serve the public with a sing-song in my voice. But after an hour of kissing this woman's ass and running around for her not like a waitress, but like a *servant* – I could feel that professionalism fading ... fast.

I looked her dead in the face, having had enough of her crap for the past hour, and said, "How do you think your cake got here? Fuckin' magic?"

with a coy smile on my lips. Her face went beet red, and she asked in true Karen form to speak to my manager. I smiled and marched into the kitchen, holding back tears. Not because I was sad; I was so damn *ragey*. My manager had seen the whole night and experience unfold, and she knew the table was being difficult. But guess what? They got what they wanted. They got their entire meal for free, except for their fountain Cokes. My manager brought them the bill and the machine.

When I was clearing the table, I collected the VISA receipt for my cash out, and where you would write your tip amount, they wrote: "In your dreams." Happy damn birthday, Erica.

Later that night, after cutting the other server, I got slammed with a birthday party. They filled the restaurant. I was run off my feet, hustling drinks and apps, because they were half priced after 9:00 p.m. That was another thing I hated about serving the corporate world: all the damn promos, all the damn time. One patron asked me if I was going to sing "Happy Birthday" to the birthday girl. I looked at them and cocked an eyebrow. "It's my birthday today too. You going to sing to me?" They laughed and continued partying. But I was still so pissed from the Alpha Female earlier that my entire night was ruined. Some champagne birthday. Cue Kid Rock's "Only God Knows Why" playing in the melodramatic second act of my life.

I didn't get home until after midnight that night, and I was completely wiped. I opened the door to my parents' house to see a bottle of champagne on the table with a birthday card from my dad.

Then I heard the door crack down the hall, and my dad came out of his bedroom, blinking sleep out of his eyes. "Happy birthday, kiddo. Let's have a toast." My dad and I popped a bottle of champagne and sat in the gazebo under the stars while I bitched about my night at work. It wasn't the blowout beach champagne birthday with a private concert I had envisioned in my head, but it was so much more.

LIFE LESSON: FIND YOUR LIFELINE

Not every day in business will be a treat. Some days you will make zero sales, have bills coming out of your wazoo, and when you look at your bank accounts, it will just look like a big I.O.U. You will have upset consumers, internet trolls, and business partnerships that fizzle. You will not feel amazing every day, and you'll question why you started your own business. These days are normal and every entrepreneur feels this way from time to time.

Having a group of people who love and support you is the kryptonite to these crappy days. Whether it is a partner, best friend, a group chat of girlfriends, a cousin, or your dad – having a lifeline to share these days with and refocus your energy to something positive will save you mentally, emotionally, and professionally.

> **Do not undersell the importance of a great support system.**

JUST US HUNTING TV

THERE WERE A few years I had multiple jobs, one of which was for the family business, *Just Us Hunting TV*. Yes. My family had a hunting TV show. It aired across Canada for a grand total of two seasons, with a third season filmed but not edited, which never made it to the airwaves.

JUH TV was all about family, friends, the great outdoors, and putting food in the freezer. It was not about shooting the biggest animal; it was about providing for your family and making memories with those you love. It really was a different type of hunting show. Typically, when you watch hunting shows, they depict the hunter looking for the biggest or most impressive animal. I can speak from experience that this is just not what the average hunter does. I have been hunting since I was eight years old, and I can honestly say I've never been in a position or granted the opportunity to be overly picky with the game I harvest. Living in rural Ontario, we do not have the monstrous bucks that our neighbours south of the border have, nor do we have the abundance of game like they seem to have. Watching these shows just felt so disingenuous and unrelatable. The animals they were passing up because of their size were animals of a lifetime for us. We wanted to watch the trials and tribulations of normal hunters – not millionaires who can afford these extravagant guided hunts. That's what *Just Us Hunting TV* was all about.

It starred myself, Mom, Dad, my sister, and the extended family, which was my dad's hunting buddies who are basically uncles to me. In hindsight, this was my first taste of what entrepreneurship looked like. My dad busted balls on this show, more than anyone will ever know. He paid for it financially, mentally, and physically, something I truly admire in him. It was not until I started my own business that I really understood what my dad was going through with growing the show.

My relationship with my dad changed over the course of the show. We got closer on a different level than we ever were able to connect on before. I look like my mom, but I am 100% Rick in personality, temper, and humour. We often bonded over hunting adventures and the shenanigans we would find ourselves in. But working on this show brought us together in a business and professional way.

I liked to consider myself Dad's second in command when it came to the administrative side of the show. Besides filming our own hunts, and actually, you know, hunting, I was also responsible for seeking out sponsorships. I would spend days in front of my laptop emailing potential sponsors for the show. Some days it was like spinning my tires on a pile of banana peels, and other days, it was like spinning my tires in glue. There were some successful days as well, like when I *almost* landed us a Ford truck sponsorship,[18] or when I landed a speaking engagement at Bass Pro for myself and my sister. More often than not, though, it was tough going. I learned a lot about the industry and was able to apply some of my Event Management Certificate from college to the business. I planned some launch parties, which were a hoot. But I really got to dig into the marketing/sponsorship side of things with the show.

---

18 I can say *almost* because we made it fairly high up at the company before they ultimately decided not to move forward with sponsorship, simply due to the filming schedule of our show. But heyyy, Ford! I'm currently driving a 2013 Explorer and could use an upgrade. Slide into my DMs ☺

The hunting industry is inundated with TV shows all looking for sponsorship. It is hard to stand out from the crowd when literally everyone is wearing camo. But we did it. For a few years we were on TV, and all the hard work paid off. We made some incredible memories and learned some life lessons along the way, like judging character (we got screwed over a few times by some partners and sponsorship opportunities), the importance of networking, and how to portray yourself professionally without losing your authenticity. All of which are some hard lessons to learn; especially when you are in the public eye.

The entire crew still hunts, some less than others. My sister and I have had families, and trying to balance hunting while raising kids can be a real chore. I was very choked up to see the show end. It did seem like a failure in many ways. It seemed like we were on the edge of glory.[19] The fact of the matter is: not every hunt is successful – which we wanted to portray in some of our episodes. But you cannot fill a season of TV with "near misses" and "unsuccessful hunts." (Unless you're *Oak Island,* and somehow you can have ten seasons of "stay tuned for next week when we maybe find something of value. Or maybe it's just another piece of wood!") We reached a pinnacle where a decision needed to be made; would we ask people to quit their jobs and travel around to hunt for JUH, or would we fold it in? Ultimately, we called it a day. The leap was too big for us to ask of ourselves, as well as the extended family, to risk it all for the potential glory and success.

There are zero regrets from doing the show. NONE. I would do it again in a heartbeat.

---

19   Cue Lady Gaga.

Here are some highlights from the show that maybe did not make it on screen:

- Turkey hunting in a blind for fifteen hours in my underwear in an attempt to secure an episode with a successful harvest. Spoiler alert – all I caught that day was heat stroke.
- Lugging camera equipment, hunting blind, and my bow and decoy across a field in total stealth mode was one of the best workouts of my life.
- Offering our autographs to hunting celebrities, as if they were starstruck by the *JUH TV* girls. I do not know if Jim Shockey thought we were hilarious or on some really good drugs.
- The hilarious stories told around a campfire of hunts long past, while looking around at the friends that became family and pouring a shot out for friends who were no longer with us.

Not only did I learn things professionally, but I also got to grow relationships with people I consider family. My dad's hunting crew are basically like uncles to me. Some have been around since birth. *JUH TV* allowed me to make my own relationships with them, as we connected on a different level. Suddenly I was not just hearing about their hunting trips, I was *included* in them. It allowed for us to reconnect with childhood friends as adults. The show provided us with so much more than just a platform to tell our stories and a cool job to put on a resumé.

I got to peek behind the curtains of an industry that is elusive to most people. I learned the art of sponsorship and marketing while dipping my toes into the entrepreneurship pool. Although my dad was dealing with the financial end of things for *JUH TV*, I was given the opportunity to have a taste of what it means to have some serious skin in the game.

> **I realized that you do not have to wait around for someone to give you an opportunity: you can *make* it.**

You can forge your own path and truly make a life you are proud and happy to live. I learned that tenacity and authenticity are my strongest traits. I learned that the best networking happens after 5:00 p.m. around a pitcher of beer. I keep all these lessons close to my heart, especially now as a business owner.

I could talk about *Just Us Hunting* for hours and write literal books on the shit we had the chance to experience. So, I will save that for another day. If you ever want to chat, I'm around. Also, all the episodes are up on YouTube. I watch them occasionally and always smile. There is no bitter taste in my mouth, just the taste of "What if."

THE BOOKSTORE

WHEN I WAS going to university, I quickly decided I needed a job to help fund my party habits … um, I mean, to fund my study groups. Right, my study groups. (Who's kidding who here? Considering my open relationship with my parents, they are well aware of the shenanigans I got into during my university days.) I did not have a car, and I didn't want to rely on public transit to get me to and from a job, so I looked to the only place that made sense: the campus bookstore.

It was actually a pretty sweet gig. They were super accommodating with my class schedule and exams, and they paid decently (especially when I considered the fact that the commute was basically free). I hooked a bunch of my friends up with jobs there too. So, working really didn't seem like work. It was just a place for us to hang out and get paid. It's one of those jobs that just kind of ended because I graduated.

While working at the bookstore, if it wasn't busy, you could hammer out some of your assignments and study notes at the cash register. It was a perfect student/work/life balance.

LIFE LESSON: SOMETIMES WHAT YOU NEED IS RIGHT WHERE YOU ARE.

I've often thought about how my life has changed since becoming an entrepreneur. There are days that are so stressful I question if it's worth it. There are days where I don't make a single sale. There are also days where I essentially break the internet due to such high traffic on the website. There are days I am exhausted professionally, only to be reminded I have to take Freddie to speech and Lauren to dance. There are also days that I *get* to take Freddie to speech and Lauren to dance.

Bear+Fox Apparel allowed me freedom in my own life. My schedule is full, yes. My cousin once described me as the busiest person she knew. That's because I schedule in both my personal life and parental responsibilities with Bear+Fox. I will run from one meeting to the next and then rush home to take Freddie to speech school, take him back to daycare and then finish packing orders just in time to pick up Lauren from the bus stop, cram some food down our throats and haul ass to dance class. When I get home at the end of the day, I'm tired – but I'm extremely grateful.

I didn't know I wanted this chaos. I'm sure if you told 16-year-old-Erica that this would be her life, she would've scoffed at you. If I knew that I could run a business and still have time for my family, friends and myself, I'm sure I would've made the change earlier in life. I fought the idea of quitting my job for a long time – even when the solution was sitting right under my nose.

THE "MARKETING" JOB

AFTER COMPLETING MY four years of undergrad in English and Contemporary Culture, I did a one-year post-grad certificate program for Event Management. I saw myself as Samantha Jones, but not as promiscuous, and with a specific focus on weddings. I figured people are always getting married, right? I wanted job security, and this seemed like a fool proof plan. When I graduated from college, I was frothing at the mouth to get an event- planning job. There was not much on the market, and I was looking hourly. I eventually found a job posting for a marketing position for a charity. The job title was "Event Marketing," which I did not fully understand, but the job description was everything I could've dreamed of and then some.

It was in London, about an hour and fifteen minutes from my parents' place. I submitted my resumé and had a call that afternoon for an interview. I was so damn jazzed. I actually had an interview for what my schooling was for! That *never* happens. I was an anomaly. I was a success story!

I showed up for the interview with my blazer, cute yet acceptably professional heels, and an eagerness only a beaver could appreciate. The reception area was super trendy. White on white on white on white with black accents along the trim. Trés chic. I nailed the interview, and they called me on my way home to offer me the job. I was starting next week.

Now, when I say I was jazzed? I was fuckin' jazzed. I had been out of school for a month and had landed what I thought was going to be a stellar job, nay, *career*. I've always had an eye and ear for marketing, and this was something I was going to dig my teeth into.

The night before my first day I laid out my clothes (black blazer, pin-stripe dress pants, and black flats) and made my lunch and snacks for the day. I was going to have a desk, so I figured I would stock up on some snacks, so I could work around the clock at my new, incredible job.

The next morning, I left the house by 7:00 a.m. to make the hour drive to London in time for my shift. I parked the car, collected my things, and walked with a confidence that I am not sure I have ever felt since, and opened the door. I introduced myself to the trendy receptionist, and she took me into a supervisor's office in the back. And that is basically when the green curtain was lifted.

The office was old 70s panelling with a generic desk and chair. No windows, nothing. I felt taken aback with the stark contrast to the trendy reception area. But no big whoop, the job was still going to be worth it.

My supervisor came in and told me to join him in the back. If I thought the green curtain was already pulled back, I had no idea what I was in for. We stepped through what seemed like the quintessential steel-grey industrial door to a room full of what I can only describe as actors. Everyone was walking around with scripts and running lines. I was shocked. What the fuck was this circus?

I was thrown into some role-play situations where the other actor was trying to get me to donate to the charity. I would reject them, and they would try to overcome my objections. I was so confused. I also stood out like a sore thumb in my business attire. Everyone else was in jeans and t-shirts, minus one other guy who was wearing dress pants that were about an inch and a half too short for him and no socks.

Then they divided us into groups, and we climbed into a car. I know, this sounds like straight-up human trafficking. In hindsight, I do not know why I turned into a total sheep, but I just got in the car. We drove to Stratford, and that was where I found out I was going to be canvassing a neighbourhood. This was not a marketing job. This was hardly an event-planning job. This had scam written all over it.

I knew the moment I stepped onto the street that I was not going to be coming back to this job. But I was stuck in Stratford with four people I did not know and no access to my vehicle, which was left in London. So, I had to tough out the day so I could get back to my car and get home.

Knowing I was not interested in this job in the damn slightest, I basically just got my steps in for the day. When the person I was "shadow training" with would ask me to take the lead on the pitch, I'd point blank say no. I cringed through the "overcoming objections" spiel when the unsuspecting homeowner would decline the invite to donate. It was basically door-to-door salesmanship on crack. We did not have vacuums, encyclopedias, or even knives. But these people were chasing the commission cheque.

Of note, I did see an old man's penis that day. When we rang the doorbell, I shit you not, a grandpa answered the door wearing nothing but a frown.

On the drive back to London, I had to hold back the tears and anxiety. I felt like such a fool. Here I was thinking I was some big shot getting a decent job out of college, and it was essentially the world's worst sales job. I called Corby and bawled the whole way home.

When I got home, my mom and dad asked how my first day went. My eyes and face were puffy from sobbing the entire drive. When I told them what happened, they were just as disappointed as I was. Not in me, but in the situation. Although we did all laugh at the old man's pecker.

I did not even give the company the decency of calling in to quit. I didn't even ask for my eight-hours' pay. It wasn't worth the hassle. I think about this job often. Like, a lot. I wish I still had the job posting because it was so far from what the job actually was. I wonder how many other eager beavers they hired that just settled into being that annoying person that rings your doorbell when you're clearly in the middle of something ... that requires no clothing.

LIFE LESSON: NOT EVERYTHING THAT GLIMMERS IS GOLD.

Including that marketing job.

I am a fairly open-minded human being. With that quality, some might think I am naïve. At times I can be, but for the most part, especially when it comes to my business, I tend to be cautiously optimistic.

If you are starting a new e-commerce business, I suggest looking for partnerships that can help you grow both your online presence/following and extend your reach beyond the screen. For instance, if you own a lavender farm and create your own essential oil, it would be beneficial to partner with a candle company, beauty product, or health food store to help get your product out in front of eyeballs. Partnering with them on socials could be something as simple as sharing their content to your stories, collaborating for content, or even partnering with them for giveaways.[20] These partnerships are always being forged behind the scenes of social media. Hold these "maybes" close to your chest.

I've had many conversations in my DMs and through email correspondence that had so much potential to truly launch Bear+Fox Apparel into the next realm. Some of these partnerships fizzle out after a suggested giveaway has low ROI. Some of these partnerships over promise and under deliver. For example, a travel company could reach out saying they

---

20   Giveaways are not always the best way to grow your audience. Be sure to partner with accounts that have similar branding, morals/values. The follow count doesn't mean they have high engagement either. Do your research before partnering with anyone who will have you. Remember – work smarter, not harder. Your product is worth more than $Free.99.

love your content and request a Zoom meeting to chat about collaborating. Before the meeting you might think it will lead to a free trip somewhere shooting content for both brands. After the Zoom, you might realize they just want you to include brochures in all your shipped parcels. Some partnerships, unfortunately, just suffer from serious "Casper Syndrome" and one of the parties ghosts completely during negotiations.

These things happen. Not every collab will be beneficial or pertinent to growing your business. This is a hard lesson to learn. I have had partnerships crash and burn, under deliver on their contracts, and I've even been ghosted mid-conversation. That one hurts the most because it seems like I was not even given the opportunity to show my business' worth. Again, do not channel your inner elephant and hold it against the Casper in a petty manner, but definitely make note.

> **Your time and effort are worth money.**
> **Do not undervalue them.**

Don't announce anything until there is a signed contract in hand and you know exactly what the expectations are from all the parties included. I have shared information before it was finalized and then ultimately had to renege on the announcement. I have who I lovingly refer to as "my lifeline," and I will share opportunities or potential partnerships with them. They all understand that it's shared with them in confidence, and that's as far as it goes. These are also the first people I share the crappy information with too – like if sales are slow, I'm stressing about financials, or I'm nervous for a new product launch. My people help keep me sane. They can see when my greys are multiplying and I've gone silent in a group chat, and they know exactly how I like my whiskey.[21]

---

21   Straight up on the rocks.

THE DECOR COMPANY

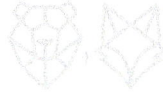

DURING MY YEAR at Niagara College, we were required to complete intern hours at different event-centric businesses. Some were extremely niche, like working alongside the events division at City Hall, or at a corporate office planning their annual BBQ. Some internships were with not-for-profit organizations, and some were not necessarily planning events, but *creating* events – like the décor company. I interned at Canada's #1 décor company for the better part of a year. I commuted Thursdays and Fridays forty-five minutes one way (thankfully, I had two other students in the internship program with me as well, so the commute was not totally unbearable) and would help the company set up the décor for mostly corporate events. It was honestly surreal. The level of professionalism and creative flair that this company operated at was second to none ... literally, if you're the number-one décor company in the entire country.

When I say décor, we're not just talking about balloons and streamers. This was nutso. We would move in entire set pieces and sitting areas, including floor tiles, carpets, couches, end tables, lighting, slip covers, chair covers, and that does not include the custom pieces made for the events. I will never forget the first time I got a tour of the facility. I felt like Charlie Bucket entering the factory. The front of the building was nothing to write home about. It was a pretty basic, whitewashed office space with event coordinators sitting at their own desks scheduling out the pieces needed for their clients.

Sarah was my supervisor and was amazing. She had a great sense of humour and, was very aware that we were doing this for free. She interviewed us and explained the internship expectations and roles we would have. I remember thinking that I was looking at the entirety of it in the white office space. I assumed they stored everything off site somewhere. She stood up from her desk and walked over to a small door, straight-up Willy Wonka style. We had to put on some toe caps (safety first!), and she opened the door. I shit you not, it opened up to fifty-foot ceilings with items organized by texture, colour, and theme. My eyes bulged and my mouth dropped. This was a décor wonderland. Literally anything your mind can think of, this building had. What did Frankenfurter say? *Don't dream it, be it.* And that's literally the mantra for this décor company. If you can think it up, they can make it.

Since this was such a quirky workplace, there were always funny things hidden in the rafters, shelves, and any nook and cranny you could find. I remember a plastic rat being hidden around the facility by different staff members. It would occasionally have a seasonal addition like a Santa hat or a witch's broom. It was always fun when you found the rat – like a good omen.

In the time I interned at this company, we set up events for Cirque du Soleil, all the Christmas décor for Casino Rama, created floral pieces to be displayed in every LCBO across the province, and even set up corporate events that were so large they had Kardinal Offishall performing. There were often moments at the end of the set-up where I'd walk around and double check that everything was perfect, from the chair covers and napkins down to the electrical outlets being hidden, and I'd be in awe of what we created. It was honestly very rewarding. I am a creative person, and this was an excellent outlet for that (even if I wasn't the one designing the décor and set-up and was more of a grunt worker.) It was a great experience all around. There were some long days; I remember spending an entire day untangling sixty-foot bead curtains. I can still hear the jangling of the beads when the wind blows just right.

Sarah was a great supervisor. She was aware of the fact that we were there being paid exclusively in experience. She spoke candidly about her experience with the company and the opportunities it brought. Me and the two other students often would ask questions while we worked, and she happily obliged. One time we were setting up for an evening event in Toronto and were sitting on a couch waiting for the truck to pull up with the last piece to set up. She FaceTimed her kid to "tuck him in," and that was a TSN turning point for me. Me! The one who did not like kids, and at this point in my life, I had zero intention on ever birthing one.

After she was done, I asked her if that was a common occurrence, a virtual tuck-in. She nodded and seemed a little softer somehow. She explained that some nights she would have to work, and that was just part of the job description. I had just started dating my future husband at this point, and the future was a very real conversation we were having. Marriage, relocating towns, unborn children – these were all regular conversations Corby and I would have. I was not sure I was ready to work evenings and weekends – which were the prime time for events to happen –because that's also when life happens.

LIFE LESSON: LIFE HAPPENS, DON'T MISS IT

I can get so caught up in my business and the constant attention it demands, such as the social media circus, the finances, quality control, packing orders, sending emails, and creating marketing campaigns, that I often worry I will miss out on the little things in life with my kids. Like when Lo learned how to ride a two-wheeler, or when Freddie finally said, "I love you too, Mom." I consciously turn my phone off when they come home from school/daycare. I consciously charge my phone in a separate room at night so I can be present with them, even if we're just watching *Magic School Bus* for the ninety-ninth time.

> **My business means the world to me, but not at the cost of missing out on our own private universe under this roof.**

At the end of my internship, I was offered a job. I was beyond stoked about this – like I said, I loved the job and the company. The logistics of taking this job were not ideal. I'd have to find a new spot to live, or else I'd be commuting alone. I didn't have a car; I was using my parents' as a loaner. I was broke, so getting a place in Oakville or Toronto was a no-go zone. It just did not work. But there was a small voice in the back of my head that was telling me I was going to sacrifice more personally than there was to gain professionally. I was young, so it was an ideal time to get into a big company, but because I was young, I had a very full social calendar. I didn't want to miss time away from my friends and family to maybe work my way up the corporate décor ladder. I ultimately turned it down. If there were different boxes checked off, I 100% would have accepted the job. I think about Sarah and the crew often. I hope they're still having the time of their lives, creating incredible events and living happily ever after.

THE YMCA[22]

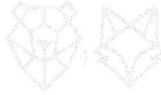

YET AGAIN, ANOTHER job I seemingly stumbled into. I was done university and was in a serious health kick. I was working out, living off protein shakes, and doing Zumba. (Who *was* I?) I would literally go to the YMCA twice a day simply because I was bored, and everyone else had summer jobs. I would run to the gym and bike for an hour. (They had games you could play while biking, so it was really just a secret way to play Mah-jong. Come to think of it, they basically had the poor man's version of a Peloton – way before their time.) Then I'd run home only to return to the gym a few hours later for my weight workout. I was just burning time (and calories).

One day, the supervisor asked me if I wanted a job since I was there so much, and it came with a free membership. He had me at one of my favourite F words.[23]

I worked the front desk, which was a very casual position. I scanned people's membership cards and was a general hub for bookings/rentals/FAQs. I got to watch the hockey games and scroll Pinterest for a few hours. Nothing overly stressful and demanding.

22　Did you sing it? Because I can't NOT sing it when I see those four letters together. Also, if you don't know what I'm talking about, we can't be friends.

23　Also included in that list: food

The YMCA was pimped out. It had a massive arena, canteen, fitness studio, an entire floor dedicated to workout equipment, squash courts, gymnasium, and an Olympic-sized pool with a sauna.

The pool kind of turned me off public pools. The sheer amount of "code browns"[24] I endured was enough to make anyone's gag reflex kick in. I felt bad for the maintenance staff. They drained that pool and played with the chemical levels more times than I can count. This is a huge reason why I prefer swimming in natural water like rivers, lakes, and oceans.[25]

I loved working the morning shift, 5:00 to 11:00. I would get a solid six hours in and then have the rest of the day to soak up the sun at the beach. (I lived in a beach town; don't hate on me.) I dreaded the closing shift, mostly because I am an early riser and hate staying up late. Yes, 10:00 p.m. is late for me. Also, spooky vibes. It does not matter where you work, nighttime is spooky time. Everyone knows that.

The upstairs gym had a set of doors that led to the track that circled above the arena. It was a pretty sweet set up for cardio. You'd never get too hot running in the cold arena, and you could keep your mind off your heart rate by watching the activities on the ice below. This was one of the busier areas in the facility. The old biddies could go and walk with their walking poles and catch up on the town gossip. One night while working the closing shift, a personal trainer came downstairs in hysterics that there was a bat that flew into the arena.

My ears perked up. A bat? Well, shit! I can handle this!

I left the desk and sprinted upstairs with a broom and a towel and walked onto the track. Two of the maintenance staff were on the track too, looking for the bat. There was some netting around the track to either keep people on it or pucks off, take your pick. I started walking around and

---

24 This is exactly what you think it is.
25 I understand that fish and other critters pee and poop in these too, but it's fine. IT'S FINE.

as luck would have it, I found the bat. It was flying around in circles, prob-ably disoriented by the bright lights and the cold air in the arena. It kept going in the same general area, just flying in small circles, totally discom-bobulated.[26] So, I snuck into that corner of the track and just stood still for a few minutes, watching it. I tucked the towel into my staff embroidered vest and held the broom like a ... well, like a baseball bat. I wound up and swung downwards over top of the bat and it landed on the track in front of me. I threw the towel on top of it and pounced. *Holy shit, what are the odds? Henceforth I shall be known as The Critter Ridder.*[27]

I brought the bat downstairs and showed off my prize. Most people squealed, squirmed, or downright screamed. There were some inquisi-tive people who were leery but curious enough to take a look at the small intruder. I walked through the front doors and let it go.

By far my favourite night shift.

But as all things must come to an end, my employment here was derailed by a major life decision: Do I move into my boyfriend's parents' house and start a life an hour and a half away? Or do we live in a long-distance relationship until one of us cracks and moves?

My then boyfriend, now husband, is a small-town born and raised homebody who will never, ever, ever, evvver leave the small town he calls home. We had been dating for a year or so and had done the long-distance thing from the get-go. It was time to make a decision. How long were we going to be weekend exclusive?[28]

He had a great job not too far from his town, and I was working for minimum wage at a gym catching bats and drinking protein shakes. The only logical choice was for me to move. I did not want to leave my creature

---

26 This is also one of my favourite words, even if it doesn't start with F.
27 I always joke that if I started an exterminator business, that's what it would be called. Relocating animals and exterminating insects – I'd kill to spend a day shadowing someone who does this for a living. Pun intended.
28 Did you read this in a Carrie Bradshaw voice? Yeah, okay, me too.

comforts of home without a job to go to. One weekend when I was down visiting him, I printed off some resumés and hit the pavement, old-school style. I dropped resumés off literally anywhere that had a door. I was open to working anywhere, but I really wanted to work at another gym. I was in the gym-rat phase of my life and wanted to continue working out for free.[29]

I walked into a franchised gym and handed in my resume. I met the AGM, and we hit it off right away. She was extremely bubbly and personable. I felt right at home with her. She gave me a tour of the gym and gave me a general idea of what the job would consist of. This was above and beyond what I expected because I don't even think there was a job posting for this place. I left the gym feeling confident, like I had already gotten the unadvertised job.

Then I hopped in the truck and drove across town to the same franchised gym, but to the women's only club. It was significantly smaller, but again, it felt like home. The manager was probably the coolest girl I had ever met. Big, black-framed glasses, pink lipstick, and she was wearing a trendy outfit opposed to the red polo I'm sure head office wanted her to wear. I understand her fashion choices; the red polo would not go with the hot-pink lipstick. It's hard to describe, but I felt something there. It sounds crazy, but it felt like a place I could actually see myself working. I've never felt that way before, or since.

When I left the gym and hopped back into Corby's truck, I told him I had a good feeling. Neither one of these places were hiring. But I had a feeling. Like Flo Rida. *Oooh, ooooooooooh! Sometimes, I get a good feelin'!*

When the weekend was over, I returned to my parents' place and told them of the plan for me to move into Corby's parents' place so we could be together. Romeo-and-Juliet style, minus the murder-suicide. They weren't overly excited about the idea, to be honest. I didn't have a great

---

29   Ahhhh, there's that F word again.

job. I was not leaving for a great job. I didn't even have a car. I would literally have to move out and take my mom's car with me so I could commute. (Remember, this is a small town with zero amenities in it – like public transit). After some convincing, my mom ultimately said that if I thought it was the right move, then I should go.

You know how when parents say, "I'm not mad, I'm just disappointed," and it somehow hurts more than if they were just to spank your lights out mad? I felt that sting. I sat in the living room just completely bummed out. This was supposed to be my moment, the "love conquers all" pinnacle of the movie. And then I heard the TV. I looked up, and there was a friggin' commercial for the gym I had just applied to. The catchphrase? *EveryBODY Welcome*. Well, holy shit, I took that as a sign from the universe that this was my next step. And ultimately, my next job.

LIFE LESSON: THERE ARE SIGNS EVERYWHERE; YOU JUST HAVE TO OPEN YOUR EYES AND SEE THEM.

THE NATIONAL GYM FRANCHISE

ONCE I DECIDED to move, it was a non-negotiable for me. Once I get an idea in my head, it's next to impossible to shake it out. I called the two gyms I applied to and explained that my situation had changed and I was moving to the area and wanted to simply follow up on our spur of the moment interviews, and they both offered me jobs. My future sister-in-law got me a job as a banquet server at a local golf course, since the gyms were willing to only offer part time work. I had, somehow, acquired three jobs without so much as a job posting. Cue Elle Woods: "What? Like it's hard."

My supervisor at the YMCA warned me that the new gym I was going to work at was sales oriented and that I would hate it. In typical Erica fashion, I did not believe him. I very much live by a "trial by fire" mantra. No matter what you tell me, I will not take your advice until I fail on my own terms. I was hired as a front desk staff and to help train new members on some of the equipment. It was my jam. I love teaching people, sharing my insights and things I have learned along the way. Hello?! That is why we are mid way through this book – so I can help teach people some shit it took me a long time to learn. Knowledge is power, dude!

I made quick friends with Courty D, another front desk employee (who I also found out worked at the golf course I was essentially gifted a job at). It made the 7:00-3:00 shift a hoot. We would create the craziest playlists for the club – everything from S Club 7, Flo Rida, and Limp Bizkit to DMX would be on our rotation. I'm fairly certain the members hated every minute of it, but it was a straight-up dance party for us. We would laugh at the people on the treadmill totally vibing to one song on the speaker system, just to change it to something totally random, like System of a Down's "Chop Suey".[30] That all ended when my training was complete, and I would work the 3:00–11:00 shift solo. It was significantly less eventful. Not to mention I'm an early bird, not a night owl.

I split shifts between the co-ed gym and the women's-only gym. I slowly started picking up more and more shifts at the women's gym until I almost exclusively worked there. Sometimes I would work the co-ed, jog to the women's gym, work there, and then jog back to the other gym and drive home. Which, for the record, would kill me to do today, but I was in my gym-rat phase. Any and all opportunities to work out were seized.

The vibe was totally different at the women's gym. It was significantly smaller than the co-ed gym. But when I walked through those doors and down the stairs, it was like walking into an episode of *Cheers*. Everyone knew my name.

I befriended a personal trainer; Kristen Stewart,[31] and we would work out together. I eventually bought personal training from her. Nothing like literally paying your friends to hang out with you. I could work out on my lunch, do a yoga class, or go for a run. Again, every job has some perks. I was the fittest I had ever been in my life. It was the lifestyle, the culture of the gym. It did not feel pushy or macho. It was just a group of gals picking up heavy things and sweating it out on the cardio machines. A group of gals that welcomed me with open arms, which was very much needed. Having moved to a new county, I was craving social interaction. These women made me feel totally at home, without an ounce of judgement.

---

30   ... WAKE UP! Shkfhsdfhjsdfna MAKE UP! (IYKYK)
31   No, not that one.

I eventually switched roles at the gym and became what they called a "Fitness Advisor." I was the person who sold memberships. I was pretty damn good at it too. I would almost always hit my BAM (bare-ass minimum) and would be rewarded with a commission cheque each month. I worked my ass off at that job.

The manager and I really clicked. We worked extremely well together. There was a definite sense of failure if you did not reach your sales goal. Hitting it felt so, so incredibly good. Plus, the commission cheque was a welcome perk. But failing to reach the goal hurt so, so much. I felt like I had let not only myself down but my boss and subsequently the entire staff. We were so close that we would all work together to help get me to my BAM. So, when we did not hit it, we all felt that sense of failure.

I made some incredible relationships at the gym. I still think back to my years there and smile. So much fun in such a small space. But like my supervisor at the YMCA warned, the sales job did start to wear on me. Then I got a pretty severe concussion while doing the Warrior Dash. That was a turning point for me. Suddenly my anxiety, that I have always had, kicked into full gear. I would leave the gym and go sit in a park and just have full-on panic attacks that I wasn't going to make my sales goal. I would leave the gym and sit in my car and cry. Once this dark cloud rolled into my head, the gym lost its happiness for me. I resigned and worked at the golf course full time from then on.

When I look back, I was definitely drinking some corporate Kool-Aid there. When a co-worker left to start her own gym, I am ashamed to say I was skeptical. It seemed like such a scary thing – to venture out on your own and be your own boss. I watched from the sidelines as Whisper created an incredible, safe space for people to better themselves physically and mentally. She was a mentor at the corporate gym, but she became a massive inspiration when she took the leap into entrepreneur-ship. She was, and still is, a huge inspiration to me and we still chat about life, parenthood and entrepreneurship often. We joke that we drank the Kool-Aid together, but we were able to spit it out and make our own damn drinks. I swore (for real this time) I would not work another franchise/corporate job again. So, I didn't.

LIFE LESSON: SOMETIMES IT'S NOT LEARNING WHAT YOU WANT, IT'S LEARNING WHAT YOU DON'T WANT.

This realization helped me exponentially when starting my business. Like I have said before, it can be a very daunting task to sit down and actually *start* a biz. There are so many variables and unknowns that it can be tough to comprehend the minute details needed to run a successful business.

For myself, it was the outsourcing of apparel. As a start-up, I wanted to make sure my clothing was quality gear without such a steep price tag that it would deter customers. I had my supplier order in different samples of tees, tanks, and sweaters. I remember sitting with a stack of clothes in front of me feeling even more overwhelmed. How would I filter through this pile and find my pieces?

I just started digging through. I tried every piece on and looked in a mirror. I pulled them, rubbed them, and scrunched them all. There were some that I immediately knew I did not want. They were too boxy, too starchy, too short, or too tight. I was like Goldilocks; I was searching for gear that was jussst right. Once I was able to narrow down what I did not like, it was much easier to figure out what I did like. I like my clothing to be loose-fitting and soft, yet sturdy enough to handle being tossed around. If people are taking this clothing on adventures, it needs to be able to stand the durability test!

This notion of weeding out things, such as opportunities or dare I even say people, by figuring out what you do not want has been very helpful. Since I know Bear+Fox inside out and backwards, I have a very strong reaction when it comes to branding and partnerships. I know immediately if a proposal fits with the company's branding and values. If an opportunity arises and it does not check all the boxes in terms of quality, values, morals, and branding, then it's an easy no from me, dawg. Every definite no brings you one step closer to an absolute "hell yes." The more you say no, the more defined your qualifications become for you to say yes, and that is worthy of a "fuck yes" from me.

THE OTHER GOLF COURSE

I WORKED AT the golf course the same time I worked at the gym. I would work 10:00–2:00 at the women's gym and then work 4:00 to close at the golf course. Close, when you are working banquets, is between 2:00 and 3:00 a.m. It made for a long day. I had Court, which always made me smile when we got to work together. We had the same goofy personality (and music taste), so we would basically just play through an entire shift. We would serve and clear tables, work in the bar, and just laugh the entire time.

Banquets were sweet because it was brain-dead, easy work. Bring the food to the table, clear the plates from the table, wash, rinse, repeat. Since it weas a banquet and not a restaurant, you didn't even have to take orders, the menus were set in advance. There were definitely shitty nights. And the tips were no hell. They were split and then added to your paycheque, so you got taxed on them. Not an ideal situation, to say the least.

But when I quit the gym, I was thankful to have a paycheque, period. It was September, so all the summer employees went back to school, which left the golf course on a skeleton crew of locals. I was able to switch out of doing the banquets and the late nights and took the open shift on the restaurant/bar side. It was not incredible pay, but it was consistent, and the staff were fantastic. I met some of my most dear friends at the course. We had a damn hoot. For legal reasons, I will not mention everything we did there, but I can tell you this: sometimes you will stay at a job that doesn't ignite your soul because the people there do, so you stick around.

It was a member-only golf course, so we served the same groups day in and day out, peppered with some guests who attended tournaments. We all had our favourite members. We knew who tipped, who didn't, what the members drank, what their spouses drank, and sometimes even what their kids drank. It was a well-oiled machine, for the most part. Mikey would come in, and I'd serve him a Rickard's Red. No questions asked. Barb would have a glass of the house white. Kathy, a Sapporo. It was a level of familiarity that was both inviting and simultaneously entirely boring. It was love/hate for sure. Most members were great. You would joke around with them, share with them[32], and spend your summer with the same people. Which sometimes would get me in trouble. Mostly because I only have one allergy: I'm allergic to bullshit.

I was working with Addie, and we were getting a few groups popping into the bar looking for a round of beer to go (the halfway house and the beer cart must have been shut down for the day). This group was on my hitlist. They were never overly kind to me. I assume it was because I was not the cutest girl there, and again, I am allergic to bullshit. Do not try to sweet talk me; I won't have it, especially if you're a misogynistic pig. They immediately went to Addie to place their order at the bar while I grabbed a cooler and started filling it with ice for them.

Our work uniforms were neon-yellow polos (the actual colour was called "volt," but I called it revolting because it literally would molest the eyes of anyone who dare even look at it directly) and black pants. Most girls opted for yoga pants, as they were not only in style at the time, but

---

32 Members were some of the first people to know when a servers LTO lead to a full time contract, when someone was accepted to university or when someone was engaged. For some staff and members, it was an extended family.

comfortable as hell. Which is a real perk when you are hustling your butt around all day serving. Addie happened to be wearing yoga pants on this particular day. Addie was a short girl with Marilyn Monroe bleach-blonde hair. She was a damn cutie. She was ringing in the group's order and one of the members piped up, "Hey! Are those see-through lululemon pants?"

Addie turned and said, "I hope not, I just paid an arm and a leg for them!" with a playful giggle and turned her back to the group to continue punching in their order on the computer.

I zipped the cooler shut and walked over beside Addie. I always felt protective over her; she was young, physically tiny, and so sweet with a hint of naiveté. I did not want her to ever feel threatened by some of the members we had to serve. I figured the conversation was over, and the group would take their cooler and be on their way. But one moron piped up, "Bend over and I'll tell ya!"

The entire group of men burst out in laughter. Until they saw me jump the bar and get a finger in his face and tell him with some appropriately peppered curse words that he was not allowed to talk to her that way and that he needed to leave.

I may or may not have actually said, "No fuckin' way we're serving you assholes for the rest of the day."

I may or may not have been written up for this situation.

But I definitely never served that group again.

LIFE LESSON: STICK UP FOR WHAT YOU KNOW IS RIGHT.

Working at the golf course had its ups and downs for sure. It ended on both a hilarious and annoying mark. That is a story for another time. But it also taught me that I do not feel fulfilled without a job, or to put it differently, without a reason to get out of bed and get dressed in the morning.

Winters when I was laid off, I would fall into a total pit of anxiety sprinkled with some depression. I had so much *potential.*[33] I was a great worker, smart, personable ... I did not belong on unemployment cruising the couch all day. I would take the dog for five walks every day just to get out of the house. We would go for a stormy walk, come home and warm up just to head back out into the blizzard to kill some time. I would cook elaborate meals just so I would have something to do during the day when Corby wasn't home. I needed to distract my brain and heart from what was happening in my head. I knew there was only one real solution to this problem. So, I did one thing I absolutely dread in the world[34]... I started job hunting.

I noticed there were lots of job postings for medical office adminis-trators at hospitals and clinics. After a few failed applications, I decided to go back to school (third time's a charm, right?) and get a certificate in medical office administration, so I could get a job that wouldn't lay me off the moment the weather turned sour. Cue the next job.

---

33   That word – often used when we in fact are not using it.
34   It's up there with laundry and cleaning the baseboards.

THE MEDICAL CLINIC

I ENROLLED IN a post-grad program immediately. Like a pit bull with a chew toy, once I have an idea in my head, I do not let go. The program had a mandatory placement component, which I loved, because unlike university, this would give me hands-on experience in the field I wanted to work in. I managed to find a placement in a medical centre only seventeen minutes from my town. I also managed to get hired once my placement was completed.

It was a weird environment to walk into at first. Firstly, everyone's name started with an "S." It was almost like walking into an episode of the *Twilight Zone*. I was the first admin to work there that did not start with an S. I naturally earned the nickname "Serica."

Secondly, the doctors were all so young. Some of them younger than me. After completing six years of post-secondary, it really makes you wonder what you could've done had you actually known "what you wanted to do with your life." They were all so kind, though. Since they were roughly my age, we were able to bond on a social level, which was great. I would come flying into work and ask them about their thoughts and theories on the latest *GoT* episode, or we would share book recommendations with each other. I never had that kind of relationship with a boss before. Even though this was arguably the most professional environment I had ever worked in, there was a personal relationship between myself and my employers I never experienced before. I loved it.

It was a busy clinic, with five docs and one nurse practitioner. I worked at the front desk, and my responsibility was to maintain flow of the clinic: put patients in rooms, clean the rooms after the patients left, book their next appointment, and complete reminder calls for the next day. All while dipping urine samples, drawing up vaccines, recording height and weight of patients, and measuring new babies. Some days I would come home completely exhausted, but very fulfilled.

Then I went on mat leave with Lauren.

When I came back it was all hunky dory.

Then I went on mat leave with Freddie. And started a side gig. (More on this in a minute.)

And then we found ourselves in the middle of a global Panasonic[35].

I did not think Covid-19 would still be "a thing" when I returned to work, but it was. I had so much anxiety going back into the hospital that I was sick. I had spent a year not overly concerned with what it would look like working in healthcare during all of this Covid-19 hullaballoo. I was hunkered down #doingmypart. I was at home with my kids, staying six feet apart from everyone, missing family events, wearing masks, hand sanitizing, and tie-dying everything we owned. I truthfully thought that if everyone was doing their part, we would be back to normal in two weeks' time. I had also started a successful side business, and I could not bring myself to think that I had spent my entire maternity leave growing a business, just to go back to work for someone else. I did not want to feel robbed of my time with my babies if that was the case.

I emailed the office manager and essentially asked to demote myself from my current position and only work Monday to Thursday 8:30–12:30.

_____

35   Like I said, I'm never using the P word ever again.

She negotiated back and asked I work Monday to Friday, but with those suggested hours.

I almost said yes.

I almost agreed.

But in my heart, I knew I wanted Fridays with Freddie. With Lauren in school, I wanted a day to spend with him alone. After taking the year to grow a business, and surviving a global pandemy, I felt like I did not have the same bonding time with him that I had with Lauren. His birth was a bit of a whirlwind trauma tornado resulting in an emergency C-section, and there were lots of unresolved emotions to work through. I wanted to regain some of the time with him that I lost during that first year. I also wanted some allotted time to work on my biz. How was I going to juggle motherhood, a part time job, *and* entrepreneurship? You cannot do everything; something had to give, and it sure as hell wasn't going to be my family *or* my business.

I hiked up my big-girl panties and emailed the office manager back rejecting the offer and saying I wanted Monday to Thursday. And they agreed.

LIFE LESSON: ASK FOR WHAT YOU WANT. THEN FIGHT FOR IT.

When I went back, it was weird. And not in the "two weeks to flatten the curve" weird. It was the first time in my life I lost all motivation to go to work. Not because I did not like my boss, not because I hated the job, not because I found a pair of shitty underwear in the toilet tank. I did not want to go to work because it felt like an *inconvenience*. It was four hours out of my day that I was not working on *my* business. The only thing keeping me at the job was the steady paycheque (which was not much to write home about since I had demoted myself and cut my hours more than in half – but it was covering my bills).

I stopped caring about the dress code. I stopped wearing scrubs and just started wearing my apparel from my brand. It was not in some rebellious nature...I don't think. I honestly think I was wearing my heart on my sleeve. Literally. I wore what I was proud of. What I thought was worthy of being worn.

I had a performance review sprung on me one day at work, and for the first time in my life it was not a rave review. My employer noticed I was not happy, that I was stressed, that I wasn't interested in being there. It all manifested in my work uniform. They asked why I was not wearing scrubs. As much as I wish I would've had the balls to say, "I don't want to be here anymore," I just burst into tears. I could not bring myself to say the words that we all knew I wanted to say. I was an A-Bomb of emotions. It was semi-embarrassing as I wiped my eyeliner and mascara off my face, grabbed my belongings, and went home for the weekend. I bought a pair of scrubs. But only one pair. I knew my exit strategy was coming.

> **I was just waiting to grow the gonads to actually quit.**

I'm sure the office thought it was about wearing the scrubs, that I just didn't like them. But it was not the scrubs – it was what they *represented*. They represented working for someone else, not for myself. It was a reflection of the cowardness I was feeling towards taking the leap into entrepreneurship. It was the security blanket of that steady income. A steady paycheque is the bribe the universe gives you to stay in the comfort zone.

Four weeks later, in a moment I am not proud of, I sent my resignation letter via email. I know it is not the most professional way to end a job[36], but I knew I needed to hide behind a screen. I knew I would be a wreck emotionally if I did it in person, and would be easily swayed should they offer me something to try and keep me at the office.[37] I gave them six weeks' notice, aware that hiring in the medical field in a Panoramic was not going to be easy. Everyone at the office was very understanding. Trying to find work/life balance with one job is difficult. Trying to do it with a part-time job while running a business is next to impossible (unless you want to sacrifice your mental health and all melanin in your hair follicles).

It was strange saying good-bye. I had made some very close connections and relationships in that clinic. I still chat with the admin girls periodically, and I have supper with some of the docs on occasion too. There is no bad blood there. It just boiled down to the most basic guttural instinct: me vs them.

That's the day I stepped out of the work force and into entrepreneurship.

---

36 Could be worse though, it could've been MSN Messenger.
37 They never counter-offered me anything to try and keep me. I was slightly upset about this, but at the same time, extremely grateful. It seemed to reiterate the idea that I was ready to move on and grow my small empire.

bear&fox

bear&fox

bear&fox

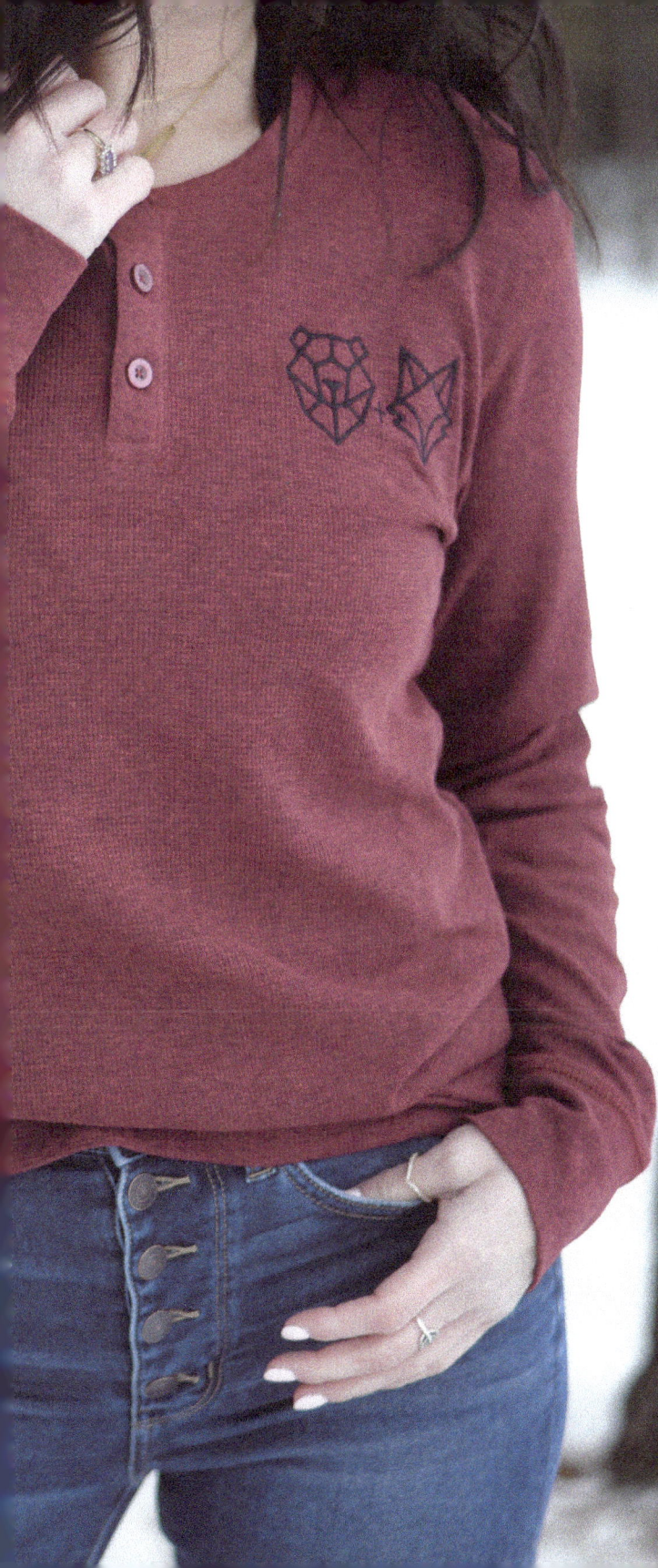

BEAR+FOX APPAREL

REWIND BACK TO when I had my first baby, Lauren. I was gifted a Cricut from my husband with the intention that I would use it for scrapbooking – which I loved doing. Spoiler alert, I never once used it for scrapbooking. Also, I am sure Cricut gets a royalty cheque every time someone credits them with how they started their business.[38] What I really wanted to use the Cricut for was creating novelty shirts for events. I am a sucker for any themed party. Oh, you wanna host a Tight+Bright kegger? Cool I have got leggings for any occasion. An ABC[39] Party? Cool, I have a sleeping bag with holes cut out for the legs and arms. Toga party? Literally, any party, I am down with. I have an entire tickle trunk of outfits and pieces for any occasion from Halloween costumes and thrift store treasures. With my newly gifted Cricut, I would have the materials needed for any shirt for any occasion at the drop of a hat.

---

38   Bonus points if you're a stay-at-home mom.

39   Anything But Clothes

I tested out a buddy's Cricut one Christmas to make some shirts for TipsEve[40] and was impressed by the product. I am a very creative person on a boring day, so the entire process from design to creation seemed doable, and even triggered the small part of my brain that is solely responsible for hobbies/projects. You know that part that says, "Yes, you should buy this random thing from this random store because you might randomly do something with it one day?" Yeah, that part.

I started making some shirts here and there for myself and posted them online. They were nothing wild and crazy, and in hindsight, they were low quality. I did not have a heat press or anything – just a shitty, old iron, so the vinyl would peel after one wash. Or the vinyl would last forever, but the shirt would be burnt by the aforementioned shitty iron. Miraculously, I got an order for a hundred shirts from a high-school classmate. And she *paid* me for it.

HELLO, SIDE HUSTLE!

Critter's Creations was my first foray into entrepreneurship. It was an extreme side hustle. Like, super side-hustley. When I look back at the name, it seems so cliché and part time. There was not anything professional about it. I uploaded low-quality images on social media; I created a subpar product (truthfully, but hindsight is 20/20); I did not do any advertising or marketing; and I put minimal effort into the entire escapade. Although there was a part of me that was taking it seriously, there was an even bigger part just thinking it was a fun hobby that generated some cash. Yes, I had some packaging and care tags that I printed for the

---

40 TipsEve – The most sacred of holiday parties hosted on December 23, which involves eating copious amounts of food, drinking too many cocktails, a gift exchange, party games, making a wish on The Wishing Tree, and caroling to the neighbours in exchange for shots. It's a tradition that has only been violated by the few years we were in a global panini.

items, but it seemed more like something you would find at a craft show opposed to something that could be a national brand.

It was, however, the perfect side hustle in that it was easily maintained when I went back to work. At the time, I was working forty hours a week at the medical clinic, which at that point I was still happy to do. I would come home and do the parenting thing, and then once Lo was asleep, I'd pull out the iPad and do some designing for my next project and still be in bed by 10:00 p.m. It was never a business I was looking to scale up. I was content with a couple hundred bucks a month as play money while the clinic paid my bills.

NOTE: A side hustle is where a majority of businesses start. It's like dipping your toe in the pool. And for some people, that's all they need! I was extremely happy with my side hustle. It gave me a creative outlet outside of work and also generated some cash. Zero complaints in that department. But you know how in the movies the main character has a yearning for something more? Just call me Moana, and entrepreneurship was my sea.

It was not until after I had my second child, Freddie, that things started to shift. The tides were turning, and I was about to find out my raft was not seaworthy.

In true dramatic fashion, I had my second baby two weeks early via emergency C-section. He was nine pounds of pure chunkable, squishy love. I was dealing with recurrent infections on my incision/excessive skin[41] and was in and out of the hospital while taking care of a baby and still filling orders for Critter's Creations. (Sigh – the more I write it, the more I am coming to hate that business name.) What can I say? I cannot sit still.

Some people are on a need-to-know basis, and I am on a need-to-*go* basis. It was not until my sister from another mister, Jenner, pointed out the obvious. She was holding Freddie so I could press some shirts for an

---

41   A nice souvenir from pregnancy/labour

order, and she said, "Crit, you need to slow down and take care of yourself." I could have burst into tears. But in true suppress-your-feelings-and-keep-a-stiff-upper-lip-Marchand-fashion, I shrugged it off. It never crossed my mind that this was too much for me to handle. You know how when you are upset and you're somehow holding it together until someone asks, "Are you okay?" and then the floodgates happen? This was that moment. I did not have the time to consider if I was okay, or even okay with the amount of work I was making for myself. I just kept going: designing, pressing, shipping, designing, pressing, shipping, designing, pressing, shipping ... When she left that afternoon, I didn't know it yet, but she had planted the seed for what my true calling would be.

Freddie was a shit sleeper. From day one. If he was our first baby, he would have been our only baby. Lo was a dreamboat in every sense of the word. Freddie put us through the ringer, over and over and over again. We tried everything to help that kid sleep, but nothing worked. When I would get up with him at night, I did everything in my power to keep the room as dark as possible in some attempt to help lull him back to sleep. I was up one night rocking in the office/craft room that tripled as a nursery, alone with my baby and my thoughts. I started thinking about Critter's Creations.

It was time consuming. There were repeat customers, of course, but there was very little repeat designs, which meant lots of extra time creating new logos and images. Even if there was an order for bachelorette shirts that said "Bride Tribe," the next order would have the same words but different fonts, colours, and even a totally different style of shirt. It was exhausting to try and keep stock on everything I needed. I was three months into postpartum life, dealing with recurrent infections, a difficult yet adorable baby, an adventurous toddler who just had her world turned upside down with the birth of her sibling, a husband, and a dog all needing my attention while I was trying to find time to make some extra cash on the side. Oh, and God forbid, if I should try and make some time for myself there as well. I can handle a lot, but this was too much.

In the middle of the night, while rocking my fussy, little baby boy, I started to dream up this concept: *What if Critter's Creations had a line of clothing with the same image printed over and over again, just on different pieces of clothing?* Then when an order came in for it, I would be able to save the time on the design and prep aspect and just print the garment. (Which is not earth shattering in any way. It is literally how every brand in the world operates. Muskoka Bear Wear, Adidas, Illbury + Goose ... all of them. But at the time it was a wild and innovative concept for me). If I could cut down some of the production time, I would essentially be making more time for my family, friends, and myself. I would be making more hours in a day. I would no longer be drained mentally, physically, and emotionally. I would be, dare I say, happier? I finally got Freddie to sleep, and I went to bed, but I could not get to sleep. My brain was buzzing.

I saw the monster.

The next night I found myself in the dark of the nursery/office/craft room thinking about this line, staring at the monster I'd conjured in my mind. What would this repeat image be? Would it simply be the Critter's Creations logo? That was a doodle I made on a piece of paper one day when I was bored. It was a cute little one-lined hedgehog – a critter, if you will. I looked at the logo and contemplated how I would put it on a shirt. It was *my* logo, and *I* didn't even want to wear it. It didn't have that ... *je ne sais quoi*. I just would not want to wear that logo around town. It was, in my opinion, unmarketable, and what the fuck did it even stand for besides my business? The clothing line needed a bomb-ass logo, it needed a name, and it needed a meaning.

Brainstorming a name for something hypothetical is tricky. I knew I wanted to incorporate my kids into it somehow, since I wanted to have a more flexible schedule with them, so why not name it after them? I initially threw around the idea of "Lo+Co." But I thought it was a shitty move on my behalf to name the business after Lauren, but Freddie just gets to be "and Co." Then it dawned on me.

The monster slapped me with its giant Wreck-It-Ralph-sized hands.

When I was pregnant with Lauren, we were those annoying people who did not know what we were having,[42] one of life's only fun and happy surprises. Whenever we referred to my baby bump we called it The Cub – a baby bear. Very on brand for our outdoorsy family, and if you know me, I exude don't-fuck-with-the-mama-bear vibes. In true second-child nature, we did not call that bump anything (but "annoying," and large – VERY large). However, when Freddie was born, he was very naturally gifted lots of fox items. I do not know if it's because his name is Freddie, or if foxes were just having a moment, much like how owls had a serious moment in baby couture a few years prior. That was the name: Bear+Fox. The more I said it and thought it, the more it made sense on so many levels.

I come from a long line of outdoorsmen – hunters, anglers, trappers, and outfitters. I am very proud of my heritage and the opportunities and adventures it's warranted my family. I wanted to pay homage to that aspect of my life.

Bear+Fox.

I also knew I wanted to incorporate some Canadiana into the brand. I am proudly Canadian, often brought to tears at a Blue Jays or Maple Leafs game when I hear the national anthem.

Bear+Fox.

---

42   I always joked that hopefully it was my husband's. I like watching the realization come across people's faces on that one. Go ahead and use it sometime. I won't even send you a bill in the mail.

The more I thought it, the more it just made sense.

I watched the monster's chest take its first inhale.

When you are naming your business, really let it resonate with you. Of course, you can always rebrand. You are never truly "stuck" with something, as businesses always grow, shift, and change. In my experience, loving the simplicity of the name along with the imagery it drummed up really allowed me to fall in love with the business and the branding associated with it. I say my business name proudly: I love it. I'm obsessed with it. Obsessing over the name helped me grow my business to six figures within the first year, because I could not help but talk about it. If I was embarrassed, ashamed, or even just ho-hum about the name of my business, that would have created an uphill battle for me in terms of marketing it. Love what you do from the ground up, and that starts with the name of the biz.

I woke up the next day with some pep in my step, which is surprising considering how often I had to get up in the night with Freddie the Fox. My husband will tell you one of my toxic traits is that I am extremely spontaneous and optimistic. It is my greatest strength and my biggest flaw. A good example of this is when I play the lottery. I do not do it often, but when I do, I immediately think I've won. I like to think I channel my inner Charlie Bucket when I buy the ticket. When they draw the numbers and I inevitably lose, it somehow slaps harder, because in my head, I was already in the factory licking wallpaper and swimming in a chocolate river. It's a vicious cycle of extreme heartache. I do not buy lottery tickets often because it is a true emotional roller coaster ride.

When I think of an idea, I just go for it without necessarily considering all my options. I don't often shop around for input from my family or friends. I get an idea and allow it to completely consume my mind, like when Agent Smith becomes a virus and Neo has to fight hundreds of him. The idea is Agent Smith and my brain is Neo. Somehow, this felt like a decision I wanted some input on. This was a big life choice! I was going to potentially leave behind my unoriginal side hustle for something a little more original but still in no way ground-breaking. I needed external validation. I posted a poll on my Critter's Creations Instagram stories. It asked if I should rebrand the biz, using some shitty graphics I made in the Cricut app with a bear and fox silhouette next to the Critter's Creations hedgehog logo. I will never forget this. It came back at a 50/50 split.

I was butthurt, not gonna lie. One reason why I do not like asking for opinions is that as much as I hate to admit it, I'm a bit of a people pleaser. Especially when it comes to those I love. Hello, daddy issues! This was the first time I publicly hinted at a change, and it was not received the way I thought it would, or rather, should have been received. I for sure thought that everyone would be on board with this idea. The fact that 50% of my followers were leaning into the idea and 50% of the followers were holding me back, sucked. But here's where shit goes sideways: *I did not care*. I had this virus swimming around in my brain, and I could not get it out. Insert slow motion fight scenes and some cheesy lines like, "For *fox* sake this virus is un*bear*able!" and instead of Keanu Reeves, Mr. Anderson would be played by Nicolas Cage.

I kept playing with the logo idea on my Cricut app. I am not a graphic designer. Through all the many jobs I have had, I've never been one of those. Although I do think Photoshop is something I'd like to dick around with one day in my spare time. (HA! Spare time, what's that?) I just could not find a combination of images that spoke to me. They all seemed so … what would Anna Delvey call them? Basic.

When Corby would get home from work, I would show him different design ideas, none of which generated much of a reaction from him. Not in a non-supportive way, but in a "did-you-make-this-in-Paint" kind of way. I needed some help. If I was going to really try and make a go of this, I needed a logo that spoke to people. I did not want my logo to mumble in a corner, I wanted my logo to kick down the door at a fancy dinner party, jump on the table, and say "BOOM, BABY! I'M HERE!"

I have said it earlier in the book, and I'll say it again: Pay someone to do the things you don't know how to do.

I took my first leap of faith. This would either be super embarrassing or a TSN turning point. What if I paid for a logo and then the business flopped? Or even worse, what if I paid for a logo and did nothing with it? Somehow inaction seemed like a worse fate than failed action. As a business owner, this is something I think about often. If you are not growing your business and taking steps to move forward, you're dead in the water. Think of a business like a shark – always moving looking for the next meal. Once it stops swimming, however, game over. Personally, my business would be a hammerhead, because:

1. They're my favourite shark
2. They're the youngest species of shark, evolutionarily speaking. After all the other shark species were out there eating fish and dominating the ocean, hammerheads decided to hunt the oceans their own way. I totally get that. It took me a long time to figure out that what I needed to survive career-wise was my own head on my shoulders.

I had no idea where to start to find someone who could help me. I had seen one business recently rebrand and update their logo, and after some digging, I found out who had done the work. I did some CSI sleuthing through their Instagram and decided to reach out to them and see what they could offer me. Her aesthetic and colour palette were essentially everything I did not want my brand to be: feminine. Lots of soft colours, rose gold, marble, soft pinks. But I did not know who else to turn to, and I wanted someone local in my corner. I also figured the worst-case scenario was that she wasn't able to help me, and she could at least point me in the right direction of someone who could. I sent her a DM on Instagram to see what her pricing would be to create a logo.

I was paying for this out of pocket. I had no start-up fund, nothing. I was just going to throw some spaghetti at the wall and see what stuck. She responded immediately. She was full of spunk and enthusiasm, which was fueling my fire, and in some backhanded way from the universe, reiterating my decision to test the waters with this business venture. When I saw her prices, it did not scare me. Honestly, I've spent more on less. This seemed like a small cost with a potentially huge return.

Opening myself up to another human being about this new business venture was also terrifying. Remember that potential I felt from friends and family members to be successful? This goes back to those gut-wrenching feelings of embarrassment, guilt, and shame associated with not "being successful." If I shared my plan with someone, and I failed – that failure would seem public, opposed to if I kept my aspirations a secret, I could keep those shitty feelings buried deep inside myself.

But I knew I needed help; clearly, my bush-league design skills were not doing me any favours.

I told her the vibes I was going for and set her loose. She got back to me the next day with six different ideas. I was determined to honour and respect the process. I took the time to really look at each logo and let it sit with me. If my gut said no, I listened, but then I leaned into the "no." What was it about the logo that did not work or feel right? I wanted to provide her with clear direction and guidance for the editing process. I truly felt like every "no" was bringing me one step closer to the "hell yes."

There were some near misses. One was a compass-style design, but it was very swirly, curvy, and feminine feeling. I did not want feminine. I wanted something bold, crisp, clean, and gender neutral. I also looked at the logos with the idea that I would be weeding and pressing the garments myself.

With my experience using a Cricut and HTV,[43] I knew the fine lines would cause headaches when I was trying to actually transfer the image on the clothing. The thicker lines would not only allow for a more gender-neutral design, but they would also be easier for me in the production process.

When I opened the sixth design, the skies parted, the choir sang, and the sun beamed down upon it. I had a very emotional reaction to it. My eyes watered and my gut pulled. It was one of those "love at first sight, can't believe they have the jeans in my size on clearance, zero-calorie milkshake" kind of moments. I knew that was my logo the moment I laid eyes on it. That was Bear+Fox Apparel.

The monster sat up on the table and looked me dead in the eyes.

LIFE LESSON: LISTEN TO YOUR GUT.

There are so many aspects of business that can be learned through workshops, conventions, and my favourite teacher: Google. Budgets, marketing campaigns, how to convert impressions to sales, and even how to make a comprehensive business plan are often courses offered at small business centres, or even online through private channels.

> **What they cannot teach you is
> how to listen to your gut.**

It can feel like butterflies in your stomach, a cool breeze on your neck, or like a punch to the chest. Your gut will communicate with you in different ways; learn to listen to it. It is almost never wrong, and almost always advantageous. I have been told time and time again that my courage is admirable. I do not think it's courage; it's simply the act of listening to my

---

43   Heat transfer vinyl

gut reaction to a certain situation. Low sales? Generate some leads by running a giveaway, launching a new marketing campaign, or see if you can find a new influencer to rock your gear. If you are willing to listen and act on those instincts, you will have a leg up on your business.

Everyone will go through different check points on their way to entrepreneurship. For me, I needed a logo to really ground the business and breathe some life into it. For others, the logo might be one of the last things they decide on after they have secured their mission, product, and goals. I knew if I had a logo, an image, a vibe, I would be able to use that as my North star, and the business would grow and evolve around it. It would keep me grounded and focused.

That night when Corby came home from work, I basically pounced on him. Good thing he's a big guy, otherwise he would've been barreled over. I showed him the logo. I just held my phone to his face and watched his reaction. I saw it. A small flicker in his eyes, like watching a match catch fire after it's been struck. My husband is rational and logical, to a fault. I was worried that he would not see what I saw; that he wouldn't see what this business could do for us, for our family. But in that moment, I saw the flame of potential burn in his eyes. He saw it. He believed in this logo. He looked me in the eyes and said, "That's Bear+Fox."

I plastered that logo everywhere. It was my cellphone, desktop and iPad wallpaper – I even had it printed and hung on my wall. It was everywhere except out in public. I was so hesitant. Putting it out there felt so scary. It would be open for judgement, ridicule, opinions. But it would also be out there for praise, interest, and it would force me to do the damn thing. Paying The Social Factory for my logo was the best money I have ever spent. It kickstarted my business into high gear. Like I said, I am very spontaneous. Before I could talk myself out of it, I created an Instagram and Facebook account and uploaded the logo with a caption that said:

"LAUNCHING JANUARY 2020."

LIFE LESSON: SET DEADLINES.

Deadlines are great if you are a list person like me. I am also a paper planner person; I just cannot get on the electronic agenda bandwagon. There is something so damn satisfying about colour coding an agenda and physically striking something off your list.

I create deadlines for myself to help keep my train moving forward. Working for yourself can grant you lots of freedom and flexibility in your schedule, which is great – until you realize it's Thursday and you've accomplished sweet fuck all. Enforcing deadlines on yourself forces you to complete tasks without adding them to the mountain of "to dos" that can become overwhelming quickly. I like to chunk out my time with goals for the year, quarter, month, week, and then day. Setting yearly goals will help keep your business on track to grow to the level you want it to. Chunking those yearly goals down to quarterly, monthly, and then weekly makes them more attainable and achievable.

It also holds you accountable to yourself. When you are a solopreneur, there is no one telling you when you need to have things completed by. That responsibility falls on your shoulders. Having your day/week/month mapped out gives you guidance and a sense of routine, even when every day is a different structure.

> Let's make this clear, everyone has an idea
> for a business. Not everyone acts on it.
> Starting a biz can be easy. Terrifying, but easy.
> All it takes is an idea and some guts.
> Maintaining a business –
> now that's some tough shit.

Growing to a thousand followers in a week without posting what the heck Bear+Fox was even about, really tossed gasoline on my fire.

I could see the monster on the operating table. Its chest was moving up and down with each inhale. It was coming alive.

I suddenly wanted absolutely nothing to do with Critter's Creations. I wanted every spare moment to be dedicated to Bear+Fox. I mentioned to Corby that I was going to shut down that account and solely focus on Bear+Fox. He was hesitant. Like, super hesitant. Like, "not even dip a big toe into the pool" hesitant. He thought if Bear+Fox failed, then I at least would have Critter's Creations to fall back on, and he was not wrong. That was a great safety net. But if you have a safety net, are you truly flying? If you are not flying, then, as the great Buzz Lightyear once said, it's falling with style.

In true Erica fashion, I created my last post on Critter's Creations and deactivated the account a week later. It sounds like some true hippie shit, but I honestly felt a pull towards my new venture. Suddenly, getting order requests for Critter's Creations was a nuisance and was often met with sighs and eyerolls. Even now, when I think back to that business, I shudder a little bit. It was all over the map, no clear path or direction. No clear brand voice. It was lost in the sea of businesses created by other Cricut owners all creating the same things, using the same images while trying to stand out from the crowd but inevitably blending in. I felt the shift. I no longer wanted to grow my side hustle, I wanted to grow an empire.

I had found my North Star, and it was Bear+Fox.

I spent every waking moment:

1. With a baby attached to my boob (growing a business and growing a human is exhausting), but we survived.
2. Designing and sourcing clothes. This was a huge benefit from converting Critter's Creations to Bear+Fox Apparel. I already had the contacts for apparel and had a great relationship with my supplier.

Jason and Michelle are gifts sent from baby Jesus. I would not be where I am without them.

3. Chatting with Alyssa about potentially launching a website. I went back and forth on this one. I ultimately decided to try and build the website myself. I thought, *it can't be that hard, right?* Lies. It was hard. I hired Alyssa to create my website shortly after falling on my face trying to build my own.

4. And of course, fretting about the start-up costs.

I ordered $500 of apparel in my first order. Remember, I was on maternity leave benefits, which pays buttons, and was fronting the cost out of my personal savings. $590[44] into a business that I did not know would actually take off. The apparel industry is inundated with options! Who was I to jump into this industry? Every business has its own financial journey and its own means to get things started. For me, it was literally whatever savings I had and my Visa card. I needed some guidance. I needed help. For all the jobs I had had in my life, I never had a retail job and literally had zero experience outside of Critter's Creations, which, arguably, wasn't going to totally prepare me for *this* business model.

I looked to another local apparel biz, Be You. I looked at their structure and how they operated. I had worked with Nicki at the golf course, and she was nothing but sweet the whole time. She opened up their operations manual and showed me exactly how they ran their biz. I can credit Be You with much of my success in terms of how my business runs. They are also part of the reason this book is being written. They could have chosen to gatekeep and not let me know anything about their business structure or model. They could've told me to go piss up a rope. But instead, they welcomed me to the small-biz community with open arms and really did talk me off the ledge about how to get my gear into people's hands.

---

44   Remember – I spent $90 on that logo!

They had a local pick-up location at a brewhouse, which I thought was brilliant! It was something I never thought of while outsourcing the product – how will people actually get it? Would I ship everything? I sure as hell was not going to open a storefront. I knew I didn't want people coming to my house to get their orders.[45] That seemed sketchy as shit. No offence, but I do not need everyone knowing my home address. Also, it seemed bush league. I wanted to elevate the brand from the beginning with some sort of professionalism. (Which is funny because professionalism was a course I barely passed in college. Especially after telling the dean that my entire final project was "a total clusterfuck.")

I needed to find somewhere to act as a pick-up location.

A brick-and-mortar store has the advantage of creating a vibe, an aesthetic, and can really drive home the morals and values of a business by creating a space that emanates those feelings. This is a hurdle an e-commerce brand needs to overcome, since obviously a website-based business does not have the luxury of a physical location. I think the Bear+Fox shop would be a log cabin, smell like fresh pine and cinnamon, and have acoustic versions of Tragically Hip, Arkells, and The Glorious Sons dancing through the shop. Pictures of cottage trips on the walls, and a crackling fireplace in the corner. The overhang on the street would be a red canoe, and the front gardens would be pine trees and one birch tree with the Bear+Fox wooden sign hanging from a branch. One can dream, right? Without the capital to open a storefront, I needed to find somewhere that could maybe get some of that imagery across.

Unlike Garth Brooks "Unanswered Prayers," mine were. A local coffee company was opening up shop in the downtown metropolis, right around the corner from me, and they were looking for local vendors to fill their shelves. Beauty! I reached out to Todd and asked if he had any shelf space

---

45   Remember: The more you can say, "No, I don't want that," the more you learn about your business. Let the no's guide you.

to rent and if he would be open to being a pick-up location for my biz as well. It took him a couple weeks to get back to me, which caused minor heart palpitations on my end, but he said yes. I might have been sweating bullets during those two weeks. I totally thought he was not getting back to me because he didn't like me, or my tone, or my brand.

HELLO, IMPOSTER SYNDROME!

But when he gave me the go-ahead, I was elated. I now had a pick-up location. A PLAN WAS FORMING! (Cue Danny DeVito dressed as the Penguin laying on a bed flapping his flippers in the form of a bat on the ceiling.)

Kintore Coffee Café was launching January 15, 2020. I took that time-line and mimicked it.[46] I figured if I played my marketing cards right, I could capitalize on the people walking through the doors to check out the café and potentially have them leave with some cozy new gear. Bear+Fox would have to launch the same day. Without that firm launch date, I might've pushed the launch off until everything was "perfect." Spoiler Alert: things will never be perfect.

You guys! I was stressing ouuut. I didn't even have a website. What the hell was I even launching if I did not physically have the merch or even a place to order it?! But hallelujah, I had a place to pick up the hypothetical apparel. This is that moment in starting a business where you need to work forwards. Many people suggest working backwards, but I never had the foresight to do that. I could clearly see the next steps in front of me, the things that needed to happen before I could move on. This can be a very overwhelming and daunting task. Trying to think of everything you need to get done in order to *launch a damn business* can hit you with a to-do list eight miles long.

---

46   Trust me, deadlines work!

One of the highest things on my priority list was images. I needed photos before I could launch. Not only did I need some snaps for the website (shit! This was still on my to-do list) but also for social media. I did not want to just shoot on my phone and apply some filters to it. I wanted to elevate the brand. If you lead with quality, the consumer will *expect* quality. So, I called on an old acquaintance, now friend and partner in crime, Carolyne. Fun fact: I met Carolyne officially at a boudoir shoot eight years prior. So, when I met her, I was essentially naked. We got close. Quick. I sent her a message and asked if she would be down to shoot some content for my bloomin' biz. She did not even hesitate. She was on board from day one and has almost exclusively been my eye behind the lens since.

> BE KIND TO EVERYONE YOU MEET.
> YOU NEVER KNOW WHEN YOUR PATHS WILL CROSS,
> OR WHO WILL BE ABLE TO HELP YOU. I'VE HAD
> SOME PEOPLE REACH OUT TO ME THAT WEREN'T
> THE NICEST TO ME WHEN I HAD A CRUMMY JOB.
> I'M NOT MEAN TO THEM. I TREAT THEM WITH
> GRACE AND KINDNESS, BUT I'M ALSO WILLING
> TO DRAW A LINE IN THE SAND AND NOT CROSS IT.

I did not know much with regards to starting a biz. Keep in mind, I did not go to business school (although I had done my fair share of post-secondary learning, with a bachelor's degree in English and Contemporary Culture, and college certificates in Event Management and Medical Office Administration), but I did know I needed bodies in the clothing. I did not want to be the face of the brand. If someone went to the website or social channels and saw one lonely person in the gear, they would think, "Why is no one else wearing this?" I wanted people to suffer from FOMO before the brand even launched. Build the hype and consumers will come. I needed bodies with heartbeats. I called on my Lifeline, who were more than happy to jump in. But I wanted more. Again, people who knew me would know the people in the photos. Is it enough to have friends and family model for you? Not if the people looking at the socials and website know that the models have a direct relationship with the owner. It does not seem genuine. It seems like you called in a favour. Then it clicked.

I invited small business owners to come and be my models. This way I could promote the businesses that made up the community while also tapping into their networks, mainly comprised of people who live, shop, and support the area I live in. It does not seem like such a revolutionary plan now, but I attribute a huge part of my growth in year one to this business model.

To this day, we continue to invite business owners to a few of our shoots every year. It helps grow their social media platforms as well. They receive high-quality imagery, and everyone gets to have a day outside networking. I know, I know, nobody likes to hear the N-word.[47] It's stuffy and boring. You picture a big conference where everyone has a "Hi, my name is"[48] sticker on their chest. Or forced conversations where you feel obligated to take a business card, even if you have no intention of ever calling that person again. But I can guarantee if you come to a Bear+Fox Small Biz Shoot, you will network in a genuine way, make connections with new people, and leave feeling uplifted and ready to kick ass.

On January 4, 2020, we held the first official Bear+Fox Small Biz Shoot. Everyone turned out. We had over twenty people/businesses show up for a business that had not even launched yet. The fact that they were all women was not even a factor when I asked. I just asked businesses I knew

47 Not *that* N word.
48 If you didn't read that like Slim Shady, you can put this book down now and escort yourself out.

in the community. It was such an incredible vibe being surrounded by so many inspirational, motivated, and determined women. We celebrated with cake (thanks, Kirsten!) and mimosas in the woods. It was a very surreal feeling. It is one of my fondest memories I have with the biz. Like wearing a warm blanket around a fire – all the warm and fuzzies.

After that, every time I uploaded a photo to Instagram, I tagged the shit out of it. I tagged the business, the business owner, Carolyne's biz See Why Photography, and I geo-tagged everything. My account grew to 6500 followers in a very natural and organic way, by networking in an authentic manner and allowing everyone to show up and just be themselves. It is a feat I don't take lightly. I never paid for followers, likes, or comments. It was all real.

I finally decided to hire The Social Factory to create a website for me, after failing to build my own shop on Shopify. Again, pay the people to do the things you do not know how to do. Your time is worth money. My website cost me $1500. I remember thinking, *if I fail, I'm out $2090. I cannot fail.* I had learned through Critter's Creations the importance of streamlining your processes. I used to get DMs on Facebook and Instagram, emails, texts, and phone calls from people looking to have apparel customized for their trips or life events. It was exhausting trying to keep track of everything. I would get lost in the mass amounts of messages. It was hard to keep straight where everyone was ordering from. I would have to search through every platform to try and find the contact information for the orders. My grey hair multiplied.

I knew that if I was going to give Bear+Fox Apparel a fighting chance, I needed it to be perceived as not only a professional brand – it would also need a professional platform for the order process. I loved my first rendition of a website. It was clean and easy to navigate on the back end. I would end up switching platforms two years later to a much more customer friendly version. Hey, you live and learn right? But you can bet your ass I hired Alyssa for that website too; she always had my back and listened to my crazy ideas. She really did go to Hogwarts for web design.

I sold out of my $500 in apparel very quickly (especially after outfitting all the models for the photoshoot, who then wanted to keep their gear because they loved it so much) and had to reorder almost monthly to keep up with demand. Every order was getting bigger and bigger. First $500, then $1500, and then my most recent order was $50k. People were tagging me in photos and stories daily. Bear+Fox had some traction.

The monster was off the table, standing and looking around its new home.

The initial tagline of Bear+Fox was **wildly local + small town proud**. You know, like wildly inappropriate. I wanted to convey that supporting my business was, like, *hyper* local. It was owned locally, printed locally, designed locally, and sold locally. Being from a small town, I wanted to make a stand that you do not have to be from a big city to be successful. As I said, my small town's population is 800 on a good day ... 802 if Gladys can hang on for the head count and Suzie can push *really* hard at just the right time. We are small beans. But do not mistake our size for potential. The tagline was printed on my apparel, on my car, in my sign-off for emails, speeches – everything. It was perfect for what 2020 had in store. I would argue it was even kismet.

THE LONGEST TWO WEEKS OF MY LIFE

WE'VE ALL TALKED about the pandemic (which will be the only time in this book I even call it by that name because I'm so sick and tired of hearing and talking about it, and henceforth will treat it like Voldemort aka That Which Shall Not Be Named) ad nauseum. It affected businesses in a way that I do not think anyone could have predicted, including Ms. Cleo. But launching a business in January 2020 that exemplifies shopping local? It was almost perfect timing for me.

The "shop local" messaging and marketing from all over the planet was hitting people hard. Wal-Mart and eBay had a shop local campaign. Hell, even Jeff Bezos got in on it. And here was Bear+Fox literally with the word "local" printed right on the clothing.

Of course, I did what every other business was doing. I pivoted (never to be said again in this book because again, I have reached my quota) and offered free home delivery for Oxford County residents. I would spend days driving around with Lauren and Freddie in the backseat literally just chucking Bear Paws and juice boxes at them so I could get the day done with minimal meltdowns. My days were punctuated by packing orders and cruising around to Disney tunes. (I can belt out a wicked rendition of

"You're Welcome" and "I'll Make a Man Out of You." Do not challenge me, you'll lose).

Sales skyrocketed, the support quadrupled, and I was in shock. Businesses were closing down around me. Alternate Routes, owned and operated by my friend Whisper[49], who was at my first photoshoot only months prior, shut their doors for good. It was an emotional roller coaster. I did not know how to feel. My business was succeeding and dare I say *thriving* while others were struggling and shutting down. I was on my Instagram daily preaching to whoever would listen about how important it was to shop local. I preached about the importance of engaging on social media, of showing support for our communities even if we could not afford to support them financially. It was liberating and exhausting. Bear+Fox became the poster child for the shop-local campaign, which again, benefitted the business. But watching the community that welcomed me with open arms struggle to tread water, I felt something. A pull to do something to help them.

I am not the kind of person to just sit back and chill. I needed something to do to give back to the community that was supporting me so much through these ... I hate that I am even saying this, *unprecedented times*. I created a purple t-shirt exclusive to the Splash Pad Fundraising committee with $5 from every t-shirt donated to construction of the splash pad. Then I helped organize a bottle drive. Then I hosted a food truck in my driveaway. Between all of these initiatives, I helped to raise $5k towards the splash pad, and that was just for my small town. I would continue to donate to other organizations such as the Canadian Cancer Society, and now $1 from every order is donated to Canadian conservation efforts. I sponsored little league teams and outfitted many businesses with custom

---

49   Remember that friend from the gym that left to start her own business? She did it. And was totally kicking ass at the private gym game when Covid struck. I think she is even more inspirational to me now after everything she's gone through. That woman knows how to roll with the punches.

apparel for their employees. I was talking the talk and walking the walk. I was living the local dream.

Bear+Fox Apparel was wildly local and small-town proud. I was elated – this is what I wanted! I wanted a brand that spoke for itself and supported those that supported it. I ended my first year blowing my sales goal out of the water. I wanted to sell $10k … I did that ten times over and then some.

If you do not think you can do it, try it. Worse case, you fail. But if you have got enough skin in the game, you won't. Trust me.

After such a successful first year, I was frothing at the mouth to take my biz full time. But I was not ready yet. It seemed like too big of a step for me to take. I needed a big push, which was coming.

I was nominated for Outstanding New Business by the Woodstock Chamber of Commerce. I was thrilled, honoured, and stoked that my hard work in building my biz was being recognized by my colleagues. I made it to the top three finalists that year. My competition was a franchised storage unit company and Kintore Coffee Company. I had nominated Todd after he opened the café in town, as it really brought some life to our "downtown." I was competing against someone I admired and looked up to. Todd and I had become close over that first year, really diving deep into our respective businesses, offering to help to each other where we could, and asking each other all kinds of questions to help our businesses grow.

Due to the Panorama, the business awards ceremony was virtual that year. I watched in my jammies, sans bra, avec topknot on my head, while I lost to Kintore Coffee. I was bummed, I will admit. I was glad I lost to Todd, but still bummed. But another one of my personality traits, which I think all entrepreneurs have, is drive. I used this loss to launch another business: a podcast called Drinks With.

Not only did I use the loss to launch the podcast, I teamed up with Todd as a cohost and business partner. Now we host Drinks With, the small biz podcast with a twist.[50] We have interviewed all kinds of businesses and have networked our butts off. It's been a highlight over the past few years for sure. It is lots of work, but it almost seems like I'm hanging with some pals and having some bevvies as opposed to slaving away working for The Man.

I continued to work for the medical centre, Bear+Fox, and now Drinks With for another year. Juggling my job, the podcast, and the business was filled my plate. Let alone the pressures of being a mother, wife, friend, sister, daughter, and human being. I ran myself ragged and became increasingly less happy at the medical clinic. The fact that I was working in a medical setting during a Plantdemic (if you turned your house into a jungle, you are my kind of people) didn't help either. More importantly, I was not giving Bear+Fox my full attention. After such a successful year and being nominated for Outstanding New Business in 2021 (and making it to the final round only to lose again), I knew what was coming. Just like I cut the safety net of Critter's Creations, I needed to cut the j-o-b safety net.

After I quit the medical centre, I felt invigorated and ready to kick ass. I was scheduling my days around my business. One day I would do content creation, the next day would be packing orders, the next deliveries and podcasting. It was such a breath of fresh air to finally feel like I was in control of my life. Of my business. Of my time.

The monster was walking down the red-carpet taking selfies with everyone.

And then I lost my Instagram account. FUCKKKKKK.

---

50   Listen wherever you get your podcasts!

THE HACK OF 2022

I AM NOT a victim. It was my own decision to click the link. I lost my entire Instagram account because I was duped. I had been trying to get my account verified to stop all the bogus accounts that are created around any giveaway or notable growth in my business. Once they even had the balls to take my logo and alter it ever so slightly and claim to be me. One of my loyal followers commented and said, "This looks like the Wish version of Bear+Fox." I still have the screenshot. It still makes me laugh.

LIFE LESSON: BUILD A COMMUNITY AND YOU BUILD AN ARMY

Every month I would apply for verification. Inevitably, I would be denied, and every month I would appeal the denial, just to be denied again. At some level I knew I was not going to get verified. But I had to try. The number of bogus accounts and the complete and utter bullshit businesses deal with on Instagram is insane, and this seemed like my small "stick it to The Man" moment. And hey, if I got that god-forsaken blue check mark, I would not be mad about it. In fact, I think it would help push my account forward and grow the business on the social media platform.

After I quit my job, I suddenly had more time for office work. I could now set aside a block of time to check emails, invoice retail shops, pay invoices to my printer, and create marketing campaigns, all while my kids were at school/daycare. I seemed to have found some sort of balance in my daily life. I was going through my junk email one day while replying to website contact emails (still don't know why they always ended up in my spam) I found an email from Instagram. My appeal for verification had been approved. All I had to do was click the link and log into my Instagram account and give my cell phone number.[51] HOLY FUCKING SHIT, BATMAN.

In hindsight, there were red flags in the email. But I had tunnel vision. This was something I had been working towards for a year. If I had not actually been trying to get verified, I would've just deleted it into the never-ending universe where spam emails go. But I was. And I didn't. I clicked the link and unknowingly handed over my Instagram account on a silver platter to some low-life hacker. Love this for me.

I was sitting in a Drinks With podcast meeting, sorting through our upcoming season and scheduling our guests. I had my phone tucked away in my bag, completely oblivious to what was going on with my social media account. Had I been home and accessible to my phone, I maybe would have seen the emails coming in that my account information was changed.

But I wasn't. And I didn't.

I took a quick selfie with Todd for the Drinks With Instagram page and left the café. When I got home, I went to post about our meeting and the stellar season we had planned and had a notification from Instagram saying I had been logged out. No biggie, I thought, this must be part of the verification process. Again, I was not 100% sure what the process looked

---

51 I know it sounds sketchy to give your cell number out, but when you stop to think about it, we hand that information over readily. Basically, anytime you order something online, you are asked for your cell number as an alternate means of communication. Living in rural Ontario and having a P.O. box as a shipping address, I often have delivery drivers calling to confirm my address. So having to supply it in this context seemed like a no-brainer. PLUS, I had no idea what this process was going to look like. Would Zuckerberg be calling me to confirm my verification? I had no idea.

like. I had never been verified before, so anything "out of the ordinary" seemed extremely ordinary to me. But no matter what I typed; I could not get back in.

Bing.

I get a WhatsApp notification from Instagram. "We've taken your account. You can have it back, but you must pay us $500 in Bitcoin or it will be deleted."

My literal response: "FUCK YOU."

> **And that's when my business got the Fresh Prince treatment. It got flip turned upside down.**

The first thing I did before completely flipping shit was create a new account. I didn't want all my hard work, my constant push to level up my business and have it appear professional and legitimate to be thrown out the window with an account name like "Bearnfoxxxapparel." I needed a handle that did not scream spam. I was able to snag "Bearandfoxapparel. ca." Not a total loss, considering that is the website address. But I was resentful of the ".ca" now on my handle. It was like staring at a massive zit in the middle of your forehead on picture day. Embarrassing. It was a reminder that I got duped. I fucked up. And now I was sitting with a new account, no content, and zero followers.

I desperately tried to get the old account back. I had to send in hostage-type photos. I am not even lying here. It was my face holding up a piece of paper with the account name and a special code emailed from Instagram.

Denied.

I would fill out a form telling Instagram exactly what happened, with screenshots of everything.

Denied.

Instagram made me send in a selfie video to authenticate that it was my account.

Denied.

My face holding up a piece of paper with the account name and a special code emailed from Instagram, yet again.

Denied.

I was beside myself. I felt rage, depression, anxiety, desperation, anger, panic, rage, rage, rage, and more panic. 6500+ followers, gone. All my content. My DMs, which had mailing addresses to some canuck celebs that wore my gear ... everything. Gone.

The monster was laying on the floor with a white chalk outline around it.

But from the ashes rose a phoenix, or whatever inspirational motif you would like to envision. I was not about to let this shit situation end my business. Instagram was where 91% of my sales were derived from, but it *was not* my business. My business is more than just Instagram and reels. It has a mailing list, website, TikTok, Facebook, and tangible, actual people.

And the community rallied.

They found me on my new account and shared the ever-loving shit out of it. I connected with Kelly from Pretty By Her and told her everything that happened. She also grew her million-dollar business almost strictly on Instagram. This was her worst fear. I was extremely candid with her and honest about how it happened. It meant so much that she reached out. I really did feel like a giant moron for letting this happen. Kelly put my mind at ease, and I was able to share my experience with her and maybe help prevent this from happening to her. Bless her damn heart. She held a giveaway for $100 to PBH: all you had to do was follow my new account. My account was flooded with new followers who had never heard of Bear+Fox before. Tim Rozon from *Schitt's Creek* shared my new account.

When I say the community rallied? IT RALLIED. I am forever grateful for everyone who filled out forms, reports, and shared my account. My goal is to get to 10k post-hack. I'm almost there now.

The monster takes a big inhale.

Out of the ashes rose the phoenix – or a monster. Due to the hack, I was able to take a step back and really look at what Bear+Fox had become. When someone would ask me what the business was about, it was not a quick twenty-second elevator pitch. It was a five-minute spiel. It was trying to be so many things:

- Support local
- Be proud of what small towns can produce
- Be Canadian
- Be outdoorsy – don't forget your heritage!
- Be size inclusive
- Be a voice for small businesses

It was too damn much. Plus, I had inadvertently become the face of the business. When I started Bear+Fox, this was something I did not want to happen. Remember that photoshoot with twenty local businesses so I could *avoid* being the only person wearing the gear? When you're a one- woman show, it's bound to happen. But when I think back to my grid on Instagram, it had my face plastered all over it. Reels. Photos. Lives. Everything. Was I more upset that I lost the account because of the business or because of what it meant to Erica?

Call a therapist, we have some serious unpacking to do.

I was given a tabula rasa to rebuild the account and subsequently the brand voice. I realized I wanted the brand to go back to its initial roots. I wanted it to be the first thing people packed when they went to the cottage, hunting, camping, on a hike or a fishing trip. I wanted it to thrive outside. I wanted it to be a national brand. If I used the word "local," was

I putting a geographic cap on its potential? I did some soul searching. I chatted nonstop with the Lifeline, Carolyne and Alyssa, to try and find the voice I lost in translation. After lots of reflection, asking myself hard questions, and facing the reality I had built, I found it.

BEAR+FOX APPAREL –
WITH YOU, WHEREVER YOU GO

Bear+Fox is your Canadian outdoor lifestyle brand. It is high quality, livable clothing that is ready for whatever you want to do. Its unisex fit allows for maximum movement and comfort. Whether you are at the cottage, camping, hiking through the mountains, fishing, or just crackin' some beers around a campfire with some buddies, Bear+Fox Apparel is with you, wherever you go. All the items are playfully named, giving a nod to this great country we call home. Bear+Fox Apparel is proudly Canadian owned, operated, designed, and printed, with aspirations to be 100% Canadian.

The monster jumps off the bed, puts on a Canuck Dinner Jacket, cracks a beer and eats a poutine.

I've grown a six-figure business on my own. I've stumbled. I've fumbled, and I've damn well fallen flat. There were many times I could have quit. But I didn't. I used it to fuel the fire and give CPR to the monster I have built. I have shipped to every province in Canada. I have six wholesale locations, including one all the way out in Osoyoos, BC (buy a vowel much, eh?). I have been nominated for Outstanding New Biz two years in a row by the Woodstock Chamber of Commerce, nominated for the RBC Woman of Influence award, and am now a keynote speaker addressing women in business about how they can build a goddamn empire.

If I had told fourteen-year-old Erica that she would one day leave Harvey's Serving Swiss Chalet and go on a wild, twenty-year ride of jobs to end up believing in herself and starting her own business, fourteen-year-old Erica would've tilted her head to show her silver crucifix earrings from Ardene and said, "I believe in you, and I'll need Sundays off."

THIS IS NOT THE HOW-TO SECTION ON HOW TO BUILD A BIZ

LIKE I TOUCHED on in the intro, this is not a book on how to build a business. I truly believe each business is like a fingerprint. They are all unique, with different models, intentions, goals, and daily activities. How could someone sit down and be like, "Follow these steps, and you will build a successful business"? To me, it is just not realistic. I'm just here to tell you what worked for me. How I managed to grow a business without any fancy business degrees, stuffy suits, or briefcases. How I organically grew my social media following from zero to over 30k across platforms. This is just how it happened. And these are just some things I have learned along the way.

SOCIAL MEDIA

This is something that many business owners struggle with. Everyone wants to go viral and explode their business. I am here to tell you it's okay to slowly grow your following. It allows your business to grow at a rate you can actually maintain. Imagine this: you upload a photo, reel, TikTok, tweet, whatever – and it goes viral. Millions of views, comments, shares, and the orders just start flooding in. Incredible! You are making money!

You sell out of all your stock, and you are staring at bare shelves. Good for you, you can pay your bills!

Except now you have people looking to place orders, and you have no stock. You are completely overwhelmed because you have so many orders to pack and ship, and you have no time to maintain your social media presence. You are working long hours fulfilling the orders, but you still need to sleep and have a life – in my case, parent my kids. After working a seventeen-hour day, you go to bed and sleep in. (Hey, you deserve it; you worked your butt off!) You wake up to find terrible comments and reviews on your social media, Google reviews, and emails. People want their product *now*. You are taking too long to fulfill the orders. You have nothing in stock. When you place your order, it is backordered and won't be here for a month. Can you survive a full month with no orders coming in? Can you survive the internet trolls, mentally, professionally, and financially? If you cannot, you risk losing a grasp on your business. Or potentially losing business completely.

Of course, this is maybe a worst-case scenario. There are many businesses that go viral and survive. Ponyback Hats is a great example of this. I am not blind; going viral has its perks. However, there are many businesses that get overwhelmed and then have more work and backlash to deal with than if they grew slowly in a way they could manage and effectively scale.

Let's look at bearandfoxapparel on TikTok. I have had three viral videos on that page – some as low as 500k views, with the best performing at 4 MILLION VIEWS. These three videos generated 18,000 followers to the page. From the outside looking in, Bear+Fox Apparel has just gone viral and the orders will be flooding in. If you thought that, you would be incorrect.

I have a fairly simple social media policy: if someone is wearing Bear+Fox, it gets an automatic reshare. If it's quality and fits the overall vibe and mission of the biz, it gets a spot on the feed. For TikTok, if anyone is wearing Bear+Fox, it has potential to be created into a video. The beauty of an apparel business is the marketing can be quite wide and simplistic: as long as the gear is in the video, it's shareable. My first viral video was a video of myself and my son when he was about six months old. We were lying together on the bed, and he was mimicking me when I made a sound. I turned the camera on and impersonated the Viking cry in Led Zeppelin's "Immigrant Song," and he fuckin' nailed it. He nailed it! I sent the video to family and friends, and we all had a good chuckle. I had just signed up for TikTok and uploaded it as a toss-away video. I thought it was cute, I was wearing the Campfire Crew, and it fit the profile. Boom. Millions of views, comments, and likes. *Pardon moi?*

Revenue generated: minimal.

My second viral video was also a fluke. We were having a campfire at a buddy's house, and we needed to split wood. My girlfriend asked if she could try because she had never tried it before. She was handed an axe and a couple of logs. I turned the camera on since she was wearing multiple pieces of Bear+Fox. She took a swing and narrowly missed her foot. There was some nervous laughter, and I turned the camera off. Off camera she was taught the proper technique and successfully split her first piece of wood. I uploaded it thinking, *no one will care about this video but it makes me chuckle, and she is wearing Bear+Fox.* Boom. Millions of views, comments, and likes. Again?

Revenue generated: minimal.

Accounts that have ripped that video off? MANY. Disclaimer: You can use someone's video if you explicitly ask to use it. Or if you really want to use it, and they have enabled the stitch/duet features, use that. I get people sending me this video being shared on different Redneck Meme accounts, with zero credit. It drives me nutso. So please, ask for permission before you share. Not only is it common courtesy, but it goes against community guidelines not to. But I digress.

My third viral video was yet again a fluke. I uploaded a video talking about an incident that happened to my daughter at school. Nothing overly crazy, but something I found comical. (She may or may not have called some kids little fuckers on the playground after they threw a snowball at her.) I was wearing Bear+Fox in the video – since it is almost exclusively what I wear – and uploaded it. Boom. Viral yet again. The comment section was hilarious too, by the way, with stories from other parents of what their children said and did in public.

Revenue generated: minimal.

Going viral does not mean your business will blow up. It also doesn't mean that people who follow you will actually care about what you're selling. They are following you for that specific type of content they liked, not for whatever else you're posting about. So, for me, because TikTok has no idea what my page content is really about because it's all over the map, my average views are somewhere around four hundred.

I personally think I've had better videos in terms of brand voice and marketing – but they haven't performed as well as those three videos. The 18k followers is nice, but it does not mean you have 18,000 people looking at every video and consuming all your content. It does, however, help when you are approaching other businesses or content creators to collaborate with you for content or giveaways. Do not discredit the number of followers you have on your social media platforms. People say the number does not matter, but let's be honest – it does.

When I lost my Instagram account, I had close to 7000 followers. When I created the new account, I had managed to retain 4500 followers. It's impressive to have a 65% retention rate (thanks to Kelly, from Pretty By Her, for a huge portion of the followers I got in that first week), but it's not the same number. Why am I stuck on a number? Well, here is some simple math for you – which is giving me anxiety because, like I mentioned, I was never good at math. But here we go.

This is social media math and applies to everyone and every account, whether you are trying to build a business, an influencer account, or just use social media to share pictures of your kids with your friends and family. Take a look at your follow count. If you have 1000 followers, you should hypothetically be getting 1000 likes, comments, or views on every post you put up. But that's not the case. The average engagement rate on Instagram is 1%. So, if you get ten likes on a photo with 1000 followers, you are in that 1%. Now, if you have 10k followers and you only have 1% engagement rate, that is 100 accounts reached. But Erica, who gives a shit? Replace the word likes/accounts reached with sales made. Now it matters. It is just basic math:

Follow count + engagement rate = potential sales

The follow count and engagement rate ratio are not so simple. You can have a low follow count, but a high engagement rate, which can still be profitable in terms of sales. The more people who are listening and interacting with your content, the more likely your message is going to be heard and acted upon. Engagement does not just have to be on your posts/reels. It can be in your stories as well. Ask your followers a question, and then engage with them in the DMs. Your engagement rate is where you will make the connections with your followers/community and what will allow you to grow your business organically authentically.

So how the heck do you build a community?

Put the *social* back in social media, and you will see your biz shift and grow. Don't think of social media as a necessary evil. Think of it as an opportunity to listen to your consumers, clients, and followers. What do they resonate with? What do they like? Create more of that. I often get other businesses in my DMs asking how I did certain things, like, "How did you make that TikTok? Who is your contact at the radio station? Who did you chat to about billboards? How did you start a podcast?" And you know what? I answer all their questions. No gatekeeping here. Literally. You want to know something? Send me a message on Instagram at bear-andfoxapparel.ca. I will answer you honestly and give you all the information I have gathered.

That being said, respect the process. I can't just give you the answers and have you expect that what worked for me will work for you. Like I said, every business is unique.

Find people, brands, processes that work for you and your business. I love pairing with like-minded businesses and people because it makes sense. Our respective followers will naturally engage with the other community if they are aligned. Do not chase accounts with high follow counts for your next giveaway. If there is no engagement on that account, they might have gotten those followers in inauthentic ways.[52] Yeah. I know, it's wild, but people will actually pay for followers, likes, comments, and shares. Especially if they are in the influencer field. This was brought to my attention by a local influencer, and let me just say, wow. Do not do this. Buying followers can affect your engagement. Since the follower you've paid for is more than likely a bot, it won't engage in your content, which affects your analytics. Just don't do it, full stop.

CONFIDENCE

Spoiler alert – no one is born confident. We learn confidence through our life interactions and experiences. Of course, we can build confidence, but no one is inherently born confident. Wow! Look at that baby drool! She sure is confident!

I consider myself an extrovert and often am perceived that way by the people I meet. I have been described my whole life as a loud person.

---

52 If you exchange money for engagement/followers – that's not a true organic growth. Nor is it a quality follower, and it can actually affect your engagement rate.

As I mentioned, I once was described by a classmate in university as "the girl with the hearty laugh." I have been shhh'd by teachers my entire life. However, do not confuse being an extrovert with being confident. Just because someone speaks with conviction and a loud voice, or seemingly has physical presence, does not mean they are oozing confidence from every pore. That person can still suffer from imposter syndrome.[53] More than likely, they do.

Every person who is looking to grow personally, professionally, and financially has experienced imposter syndrome. Imposter syndrome is like the last person at the party who just will not get the hint to *leave*. They creep into the party, uninvited, drink all your booze, lick their nachos before they dip them in the taco dip, and then stay well past last call. There's the door, bud, get the fuck out.

Imposter syndrome manifests itself in different ways for different people. But it has the same bottom line: it scares people away from what they want to do. It stops them from:

Launching that business

Starting that Instagram account

Talking to that person

Posting that video

Trying literally anything new

It stops you. Point blank, end of discussion.

Imposter syndrome basically whispers in your ear, **WHO DO YOU THINK YOU ARE?** It causes doubt in ourselves. I did not experience this much when launching Bear+Fox – but I have experienced it almost daily since I took the biz full time. When I started the biz, I was nobody and therefore had nothing to lose (except $2000.) Or at least that is how I saw

---

53   Imposter Syndrome – the nagging feeling that your successes are not because of your hard work and that you don't deserve what you've worked for.

it. As the business grew, and my recognition in the community grew, that is when the whispers started. Suddenly I felt like I had something to lose. The risk of failure was a constant whisper in my ear. I would lose sleep over the most ridiculous notions. *Why am I thinking about the caption on that TikTok instead of sleeping?* It happens to the best of us. I've learned the best way to deal with imposter syndrome, and it's literally the simplest counterattack. When the whisper of doubt questions your actions, *answer it.*

I've been facing imposter syndrome while writing this book. BIG time. It has been whispering in my ear from the moment I sat down and opened my laptop. It whispers in my ears when I'm showering, walking the dog, playing with my kids, and during my Instagram Lives. It is basically the second cousin to a Dementor[54] – a cold, unfeeling ghost-like creature that sucks all the power and confidence out of me with one small question:

WHO DO YOU THINK YOU ARE?

I have learned to battle the Imposter Dementor. Not with the Patronus Charm, but by simply answering the question. This is literally what happened to me last night.

Past Erica: I'm going to start a new Instagram page. A place where I can promote this book and share some business strategies with other users and keep the branding of Bear+Fox Apparel separate.

Imposter Dementor cracks a window and slithers in on the cold breeze. It slinks behind my wingback chair and tucks my hair behind my ear with its cold, bony finger. It leans in close enough that I can feel its breath.

Imposter Dementor: WHO DO YOU THINK YOU ARE?

---

54   If you don't understand this reference, you need to educate yourself. Or we can't be friends. #pottheadsforever

Past Erica: Who am I? I'm Erica Marchand, CEO/Founder of Bear+Fox Apparel. I grew a six-figure business in my first year with no business experience. I grew an authentic and incredibly strong social media community. I survived a hack. I have shit to say. Who the fuck are you?

Imposter Dementor slouches its shoulders and begrudgingly shows itself out the front door.

I find answering the question and not letting it sit and stew in my mind helps to keep me focussed and on track. It is very easy to compare ourselves to others. This is what feeds that notion that we are not good enough, that we are not worthy of success. If we answer the question imposter syndrome poses, then it holds no power over us.

Don't be afraid to start something and take that leap just because some asshole in a cloak is whispering bullshit in your ear.

SUPPORT SYSTEM

I could not have taken the plunge into entrepreneurship without my support system. Let's be clear, I'm saying support *system*. They say it takes a village to raise a child – well, it takes a damn network and community to build a business, even if you are a one-man show. There are three main pillars that create a support system:

OUTSIDE SUPPORT
SUPPORT FROM YOUR CIRCLE
SUPPORT FROM WITHIN

Outside Support: Todd from Kintore Coffee has been a huge supporter basically from the moment Bear+Fox Apparel launched. We have weekly meetings for our podcast, and we always make the time to ask about each other's businesses, touch base, and see if there is anything we can do to support one another. Sometimes it is just lending an ear and listening to what the other person is working through. Sometimes it's celebrating the other person's successes. Sometimes it's just having a beer with someone else who has the entrepreneurial spirit[55] and kind of "gets it."

This is one of the beautiful things about the Drinks With podcast. We get to meet and chat with so many different business owners at so many different levels of business. It is such an incredible feeling to hear that someone with a million-dollar business can relate to something you're going through as well. Keeping company with like-minded people can really fuel the fire. That being said, it's nice to diversify your support system. Chat to people outside of your industry. Todd sells coffee, and I sell apparel. They are two totally different products and businesses, but we are able to help each other and learn from each other because we see different aspects to each other's business.

Support from Your Circle: My husband is co-owner of a civil engineering firm and has a totally different perspective and outlook on business than I do. As frustrating as it can be to listen to his rationale, he often comes at my situations/problems with a totally different resolution than I would ever consider. I truly value that. He is the ying to my yang, and we balance each other out well. I could not have done this without him. Also, in terms of support system - find someone who can pick up your slack.

Corby and I are both building and scaling businesses, which takes blood, sweat, tears, and above all, time. Sundays we look at our upcoming week and figure out who is coming and going and, most importantly, who is taking care of the kids. We do not have a nanny - we are building businesses while still being present for our family. It takes some finagling and our families have helped us when and where they can. Sometimes it takes

---

55   Entrepreneurial Spirit - that certain *je ne sais quoi* often found in self-made hundredaires. That tenacity, drive, hunger, and need to build and scale a small empire where the creator is king.

a little more planning, but we find what works for our schedules and our kids' lives, and we plan around it.

Remember when I said get a good planner? I treat mine like a diary. I write everything down in it, and this is partly because we have to schedule everything, including our spouse's schedule, outside of the family events. We try to be conscious of the other person's schedule and life and find that unicorn everyone talks about – work/life balance.[56] Some weeks we joke that we are more like roommates because we both have so many moving pieces in our schedules. We always connect throughout the day, and Sunday morning coffee dates are my favourite. We know this is a small moment in time and often dream of the day our businesses can run without us being there facilitating the gears into motion. It will all be worth it then. I could not have done this without Corby, and I know that. I thank him daily for it.

Family and friends are part of that inner circle.[57] Do not be fooled that support means financial support. That's totally different. Some people just might not be interested in what you're selling or creating, and that's okay! It does not mean they don't love you; they just aren't your target demographic. But if they support you, ask how you're doing, ask if you need help, help you pack orders after you have surgery, model for your photoshoots, share your content on social media, comment on posts, tell their coworkers about your business, nominate you for grants/awards, still invite you out to social events even though they know you're flat broke because you're building an empire,

---

56 For the record, I don't believe this exists. Some days your work will require more of your attention in order to succeed. Some days your family will demand your time. It's not finding a daily balance; it's having forethought and presence of mind to determine what is important today. This is especially important and very damn hard when you have kids. Because, you know, they need to be fed, watered, and entertained. Oh, and if you can find the time to also help them grow into decent human beings and not the next Ed Gein, that would also be appreciated. But no pressure there. Oh, and get a damn planner already.

57 Disclaimer – it won't be all family, and it won't be all friends.

bring you a bottle of Forty Creek[58] because they know you're stressed to the tits with the new Fall/Winter launch – they've done their job.

Support from Within: This is a tricky one. Not only are you going to deal with imposter syndrome, but you are also going to be faced with all kinds of shit from within. It does not matter how mentally stable you are; if you don't have support from within, you're straight screwed. There will always be moments of doubt, confusion, or second-guessing decisions – this is life. However, if you take the time to take care of yourself, you will be better able to manage the confusion and second-guessing. Everyone will have different things that work for them. Maybe it is getting your nails done, a massage, working out, meditating, walking the dog – whatever.

For myself, I find I need to schedule into my planner[59] time away from the business and away from my family, so that I can focus on myself. It took me two years of building my business to actually realize the importance of this. I was getting myself stressed out because I was not taking the time to refocus and recentre myself. Now I schedule in my workouts, my massages, hair appointments, and pedicures. These are the non-negotiables in my life that allow me to take the time away from the hustle and bustle of the biz and life in general and exhale. I also have a sheet of paper with all the months broken down into blocks, one for each day in the month. I colour in the days that I move my body for thirty minutes (I include walking the dog and walking to the kids' bus stop.) It is satisfying to colour in the blocks, and it's also guaranteed screen-free time that I can step away from the business and breathe. It might seem selfish – I get it. I do not look at it as treating myself, I look at it as self-care. A treat would be an entire weekend away to endure all the manis, pedis, massages, and soaks while my wine glass is constantly being filled and I do not

---

58   My favourite Canadian whiskey. Friendly reminder: I will never turn this down.
59   Have you got one yet?

have to answer the question of what's for supper because someone else is just going to serve me while I have cucumbers on my eyes. A massage to help with my posture and back pain? That is self-care. Take the time for yourself – no matter what that looks like for you. If you don't allow yourself that time away, and you are constantly just living in the tornado that is your biz, you will get swept away and you will have no idea of how to get back to Kansas.

BUILD YOUR SUPPORT SYSTEM/TEAM

I've always been a DIYer. If I could do it, I would do it. I remember as a little girl going to craft shows with my mother and looking at all the incredible talent harboured in the booths. I'd touch all the handmade goodies and admire the craftsmanship, the colours, the vast range of crafts all present under one roof. I would pick up a craft and hold it in my hands, looking at the pieces that made it whole. I inevitably would find myself down the rabbit hole. If *I* made this, I'd do XYZ. Or once I was able to hold something, I'd really examine the construction and think, *I can build this.*

I've been like that my whole life. I'm a creative person, and I like working with my hands. It comes as no surprise that entrepreneurship is like a drug to me – it is creating something out of nothing. In building a business, I have become that little girl walking through the craft show. I look at the business as a whole and start to break down its pieces: marketing, bookkeeping, accounting, inventory, advertising, brand awareness, quality control, and PR. As much as I would like to think I'm good at all of it, I'm not.

Your time and sanity are worth saving. If there is an aspect of your business that negatively impacts you mentally or even physically, hire it out. Pay the people who like to do the things you don't. They are out there. My sister-in-law double majored in math and physics. People can be into weird things. Personally, spending my day with numbers and theories sounds like the third layer of hell, but for Dee, the only thing that would make it heaven would be if they were serving gin martinis at a bar that looked like the periodic table.

Part of the success of Bear+Fox Apparel is that I played into my strengths early on in the business. I knew what I was good at, or even enjoyed doing (if you enjoy doing something, you naturally will become better at it because you'll be practising that skill without even thinking about it), and I focussed on those aspects. Budget and numbers have never been a forte, so I reached out for help in those regards. Marketing, social media management, and content creation are some of my favourite aspects of a business, so I doubled down on them. You cannot be good at everything, so do not stretch yourself thin trying to do it all yourself. Like that pizza dough you keep flipping in the air, if it gets stretched too thin, it tears a hole right in the middle of everything. Focus on your strengths and ask for help in the areas you lack.

PLAN TO CHANGE

Take a moment to think back to what you were like in high school. I wore heavy eyeliner, often brushed my curly hair into a too-tight ponytail, had a unibrow (thanks, Dad!), and wore my dad's old Dickies work pants and a graphic tee or the low-rise hip huggers with a spaghetti-strap tank top with *all* the costume jewelry. I listened to Weezer, The White Stripes, and all the pop-punk bands ad nauseum, and cared more than I care to admit about the attention of boys. Puberty, such a trip. Now imagine if I was a thirty-four-year-old walking into work wearing big purple plastic hoop earrings, thick eyeliner, an unkempt bun at the nape of my neck, and wearing my father's clothes. You could basically pump Bowling for Soup's "1985."

Just like people, businesses change and grow, from something as simple as the advertising campaign to the actual product as well. Do not back yourself into a corner and think you have to have all the answers from the moment you launch your business. Listen to what the business is telling you, and let the customers guide you to what they want.

When Bear+Fox started, the tagline was "wildly local + small town proud." I knew I wanted to grow the brand to be bigger than just Oxford County, I just did not know how to do that with a tagline that hyper-focussed on the notion of "local." I was able to take a step back (thanks to the scam of 2022) and really realign the brand the way I initially wanted it to be portrayed – an outdoor lifestyle brand. With the new slogan "With you, wherever you go," Bear+Fox Apparel has been able to hunker down with the niche content and really allow the consumer to know exactly what the brand stands for.

It does not matter where you live: the brand is with you, wherever you go. With the word local in the slogan, it really capped the potential for growth, outside of Oxford County. Or at least I perceived it that way. Maybe I was wrong. But I do feel a deeper connection to the brand and business since the slight shift in messaging.

DARE TO COMPARE

This is something that will destroy your ego and business in a heartbeat: comparison. It is something we all do. If you have a sibling, you've for sure been compared to them in some way. I know we compare Lauren and Freddie Joe all the time. I constantly mention how late Freddie is to speak because Lauren was such a well-spoken child. Freddie was late to walk, while Lauren was running laps at twelve months old. Freddie is destructive, Lo is not. Freddie never napped; Lauren napped like clockwork. There may be times where comparison is okay – that is why we have milestones to watch for in our children. But it can be detrimental to development, let alone self-esteem.

Think of your business as your baby. You grew it, nurtured it, and birthed it. Welcome to the world, Baby Biz! You are completely engulfed in your business and all the opportunities it will endure. And then you go to a networking event, or rather, a play date. All types of businesses are there, and you get to meet the people behind the brand. Suddenly you are comparing your business to everyone else's in there. Well, Rebecca has a million-dollar business, and I haven't cracked $50,000. I must be doing something wrong. I'm an idiot. Why did I think I could do this?!

But what you don't know is Rebecca's business. Did she have capital to begin? Maybe there is a silent partner that funded the start-up? Maybe she sold a kidney back in 2007 and used that as a down payment for her flagship store; you do not know *Rebecca's* business, because it's none of *yours*. She does not know your business, either. Stay in your lane and learn from the opportunities, events, or people who fill your cup.

Beware, not every business that is outwardly successful is actually successful. That word is dangerous – "successful." Success is measured differently by different people. Success to you might be the flexible schedule and ability to finally have a small coop of chickens, while success for Rebecca is owning a ten-million-dollar business. Comparison will more often than not distract us from our goal and cloud our perception of our current successes.

It's hard. I get it. I've compared myself to businesses (not even in the same industry) and have felt defeat. When you pour so much of yourself into your business only to see someone else presumably get all the accolades, it can really suck the joy out of your day. Focus on your business, your happiness, and your definition of success. Of course, you can reach out to other businesses and owners for advice and insight, but be mindful of that Comparison Plague - it spreads quickly and leaves crumbled business owners in its wake

HOW DO YOU KNOW WHEN TO MAKE THE LEAP TO FULL-TIME ENTREPRENEURSHIP?

THE LONG LIST of jobs that I have under my belt vary from waitressing, inputting data, door-to-door marketing, sales jobs, customer service jobs, and office jobs. All of these jobs offered different learning opportunities and chances to develop and hone my skills. But all of them have one common denominator: I was not happy.

I knew I was ready to take a chance on myself when I realized that working for other people was not fulfilling me and allowing me to live a life that I was proud of living. I was caught up in the mundane nature of my jobs, the repetitive routines, the constant dread on Sunday that tomorrow would start yet another week at a job that just, frankly, did not spark joy.

I stressed out over asking for time off to take care of my kids or for appointments because I did not have daycare lined up or, gasp, for a vacation. I am a firm believer in making memories while you can because life is short. I hated that a huge part of my life was being dedicated to people and jobs that just did not make me happy. Seeing my friends and family actually happy at their jobs gave me extreme jealousy. That was a driving factor in my decision. Life is too short to be jealous, sad, bored or unhappy – so I chose happiness.

And you can too.

ACKNOWLEDGEMENTS

I ABSOLUTELY HAVE to take the time to thank everyone who made not only Bear+Fox Apparel a success, but also this book.

First and foremost – I want to thank me. I want to thank me for knowing what I want in life and chasing it. For showing up on the days when the Imposter Syndrome was screaming that I was a fraud and drop kicking it into oblivion. I want to thank me for showing my kids what determination, perseverance, and a no-bullshit attitude can get you. Thanks Past Erica, you are truly cooler than you give yourself credit for.

I want to thank my dad – the first person to push me, question me, and support me. Forever thankful for everything *Just Us Hunting* TV taught me – including the fact that some of the best business happens after-hours, bush-league players can roll with the elite, and how to keep a stiff upper lip. Working with you would have killed the ordinary man, but we both survived.

Mom, thanks for everything you did for me through childhood. From staying home to raise us, to showing me it is never too late to dive into the work force – you are the most patient person I know. I hope that one day I can roll with the punches as gracefully as you do.

Sis, thanks for always being a sounding board for me and my wild ideas. Also, you should feel lucky I decided against an entire chapter full of "ugly sis pics" as payback for the moniker Poo Poo in the Lake Girl. I will save that content for the next billboard.

Corby aka Big Papa – you are the best partner I could ever ask for. I cannot fathom what went through your mind when I told you I was quitting my job. Or that I was writing a book. You never cease to amaze me with your extreme rationale and logic – and yet somehow, you were able to rationalize that this was the best move not only for me, but for our family. Thanks for always having my back and for the constant support. Lolo, Freddie Joe, and I are the luckiest people to have you in our corner. Same Team.

Carolyne – thanks for always answering the call. Always down for an adventure, and ready for shenanigans. #almostfamous.

Alyssa – from mentor to friend, you have been there since Bear+Fox was just a dream. Now you are here, living the dream with me. Thanks for never eye rolling your way through my tech-deprived texts and for creating the world's best logo of all time. Are you *sure* you didn't go to Hogwarts?

The Lifeline – ya'll know who you are. Thanks for helping me name the OG 6 pieces in the shop and for showing up on the socials, the shoots, and in life. It would not be the same without you. Love ya! Mean it!

KD – thanks for the lifetime of friendship and helping me with the design for this book. You know me better than I think I know myself. You are always there when I have a ridiculous story or heartbreak. You did not even flinch when I had a crazy idea for a music video about cannibalistic hillbillies, or when I insisted we watch *Grizzly Man* on repeat for an entire weekend and then learn the theme song and listen to it on repeat for eternity, or when I suggested we have a costume party for the finale of LOST. You are one in a million, kid, and I wouldn't have it any other way. Sweet Dreams.

Brooke – thanks for being the first person to share a daytime bevvie with, to share Bear+Fox across socials, and to order every product I have ever carried. You are the best forced friendship. Also, thanks for rubbing out that Charlie horse I had our first night in residence. To leap out of bed and rub someone's calf you do not know while they scream in agony, that is a good person right there.

BK – you are an excellent cheerleader and you never judge the state of my baseboards. Your snapchat Bear+Fox hauls are always a crowd pleaser. #influenceme

To everyone who came to the very first Bear+Fox photoshoot. You agreed to come and support myself and my biz before we even officially launched. I attribute so much of my success to you and your willingness to welcome me to the community. And yes, everyone gets a shout out:

- Alyssa – The Social Factory (the very one who designed my website and logo)
- Kate – Early Bird Coffee
- Kirsten – KYND Beauty Spa
- Mike – Kirsten's boyfriend (and the only dude present and accounted for at this shoot)
- Alex – Azalea Yoga
- Whisper – Alternate Routes
- Kendra – Kay+King
- Rhonda – Brandow Soap Co.
- Erin - Stampopotamus
- Kirsten – Cakes by K (she even made a cake and cake pops to celebrate!)
- Aurora – Perfect Pineapple (she is literally thirteen and killing the scrunchie game!)
- Christina + Becky – Workshop Supply
- Kendra – Revoilutionary Wellness

- Dee – Sister-in-law extraordinaire
- BK – friend to the end
- Jenner + Taz – The Tribe
- Holman – Lifeline (who has since started her own business, Noods Pasta)
- Kait – Lifeline (who since has since started her co-owned business, Glasshouse Cosmetics)

Todd from Kintore Coffee – thanks for being one of my support pillars. From café chin wags to podcast night caps, we seem to solve all the world's problems over a pint or two. I will gladly lose to you any day, Pearson!

To all my employers from all my jobs – thanks for the life lessons.

And lastly, thanks Mrs. Westbrook for fueling my temper tantrum in Grade 10 math class. It took twenty years, but I am finally a published author.

ABOUT THE AUTHOR

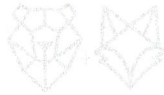

ERICA MARCHAND grew up in the outdoors in rural Ontario, hunting, trapping, and fishing with her family. This love of small-town Canadian life would eventually become the inspiration for her apparel company Bear+Fox, which is named after her kids. She has a bachelor's degree in English and Contemporary Culture and college certificates in Event Management and Medical Office Administration. She lives in Embro, Ontario, with her husband, their two children, their dog George and cat Eddie.

For more information about Erica and Bear+Fox, see:
www.bearandfoxapparel.ca
instagram: bearandfoxapparel.ca
facebook: bearandfoxapparel
tiktok: bearandfoxapparel

CPSIA information can be obtained
at www.ICGtesting.com
Printed in the USA
BVHW062145070123
655773BV00003B/13